Reviews

"An inspiring read.

This book, Attaining Personal Freedom, blasts through common ideas about what living an ideal life actually means. Teaching us that good enough is not enough as we bear intimate narrative witness to the reality that the souls journey never ends. The tales accounted between these pages demonstrate that with steadfast honest work a joyful life of integrity is within our reach. Whatever your starting point, stable transformative growth is possible.

Truly out of the box accounts of transformation which are remarkable in their scathing honesty & juicy untethered freedom.

We are enticed to go beyond what one could hope to shop for at the latest wellness fair. In making the commitment to boundless self-growth we discover through these examples that a purposeful life of wonder is our shared birthright."

Nicole T.H. Tait ~ Mother & Artist at Corvus Nest

"In "Attaining Personal Freedom-Intimate Journeys of Courage", Tanja Diamond and her coaches tell of their raw, vulnerable, truthful journey. These amazing accounts are simultaneously awe inspiring and intense. And yet the gratitude expressed by Tanja's coaches is testimony to the power and freedom in the work. Tanja's "High Speed Evolution" course cuts the non-sense out of the personal growth industry and delivers practical straightforward methods for attaining personal freedom. I highly recommend this book for anyone who seriously desires a vibrant awakened life."

Doug Sparks- Sufi Teacher, 5Th Dan Aikido Sensei

"Tanja Diamond's "Attaining Personal Freedom – Intimate Journeys of Courage" is a tantalizing sprint down the pathways of the personal growth of her first certified coaches.

It transcends "self-help"; instead exploring the mental, spiritual and emotional twists and turns they each take to finding their way back to themselves. Each journey is different; as different as each of the individuals.

But no question as to the depth of each journey and how they each found parts of themselves they didn't know existed before and desires and passions that had laid dormant their entire lives. It opens your heart to question your own goals, life plans, needs and values... indeed, even who you are!"

Melody Brooke- Marriage and Family Therapist
www.melodybrooke.com

"If as you are reading this book you feel resistance, consider yourself blessed to be on a life altering path. That resistance is your edge of growth.

Beyond the tears of frustration and joy that inevitably flow when you choose to immerse in Insourcing, as Tanja calls it, is a life lived in total awareness of your true values and purpose. Her methods are unconventional and at times maddening, but always grounded in compassion. Her coach's stories will inspire you. These women are courageous, vulnerable, authentic and wise. Keep reading. Find your courage. Do the work. Feel the shifts."

Tina Bernard- Sales Executive and High Speed Evolution graduate

"Tanja, I'd like to be one of your coaches!

"Attaining Personal Freedom - Intimate Journeys of Courage" takes you into the inner world of 4 women who are going through an awakening, as they journal through the details of the personal development program "High Speed Evolution" that Tanja teaches.

Reading this book allows you to observe their deep introspection as they navigate new terrain and integrate unique practices into their daily lives. It was inspirational but also educational as I learned more about the NLP technique Pattern Interrupt, why and how it works, and so much more mind-blowing information.

I'm so glad I read this book as I could relate to all 4 of their life experiences in different ways and it caused me to pause and reflect on how I could do things differently myself and achieve these same results. Becoming aware of what is holding us back and how we can put ourselves in the driver's seat of our lives.

What a wonderful tribe of empowering women Tanja has gathered, it was beautiful to see how they supported and held space for each other during crisis.

Overall this book helped me to visualize bright future possibilities and to see the journey as valuable, as the women learned to feel ALL THE THINGS, to notice what is out of alignment, what the lesson is, and ultimately being okay with the emotional aspect of our humanity."

Chantelle Neufeld ~ Hypnotherapist and Counselor
www.chantellen.com

"This book is a most worthy addition to the small collection of truly-valuable self-help/spiritual-journey narratives.

What sets these narratives apart from the mass of spiritual memoirs is the personalness, the nuance, and the sense of hopefulness in these women's stories. They have suffered profoundly, and yet found expansiveness & meaning in an inner freedom that is not contingent on belonging to a religion or in the reflected glory of a guru. Each voice is very different, and it's deeply moving to read of each one's journey from desolation into a full aliveness and sovereignty. Their descriptions of the spiral nature of unfoldment and the inevitable pitfalls and obstacles attendant to fully claiming oneself are deeply touching and poignant, and the universality of their overall experience inside the specificity of each woman's struggles and triumphs is rich and nourishing.

Tanja's description of how we become enmeshed in our personal prisons and the nature of the human conundrum — is exquisite and so very true. Her writing is clear and uncluttered, concise, and her approach straightforward. If her description of our mental machinery seems simplistic, it's also very useful in its simplicity — and we all need some kind of framework through which to understand and navigate our interior process when life is functioning in breakdown mode.

I don't agree with every point she makes — but it's not necessary that I do. There are different teachers and different teachings because there are different students, and there is a cosmic choreography at work that brings the student to the right teacher "in the fullness of time," as they say in the East. I am honored to have been asked to write this review, and can't wait to refer friends and other seekers to this volume."

Hafizullah is a Sufi shaikh based in Seattle and guides students all over the world in the alchemy of inner freedom.

ATTAINING

PERSONAL

FREEDOM

Intimate Journeys of Courage

Thank you, Bev, Donnaah, Robyn and Keli for your courage to make this book a reality and carrying on my legacy.

Thanks to Lyric my doppelganger, laughing healer and co-conspirator, you kept me sane LOL

"Attaining Personal Freedom – Intimate Journeys of Courage" copyright 2018

Tanja Diamond. First edition published March 2018.

All rights reserved published by Modern Tantra Press

Cover Concept and Design- Tanja Diamond

Cover photoshop work- Jonathan Roumain www.Ro2.ca

Book Formatting-Suzette Vaughn

Publisher- Modern Tantra Press

ISBN-13: 978-0-692-07762-7

Published In the United States

Medical and Therapeutic Disclaimer:

The advice and exercises in this book can and will change your life. You should be prepared for this. There can be big emotional shifts that occur. Common sense and good judgment should be used for both the physical and emotional aspects presented.

This book is for informational purposes only. It is not a substitute for medical care or psychotherapy. If you are in need of medical care or psychological counseling, please see a licensed professional. Follow the advice of your health care provider if you are in treatment.

Dedication

This book was written during one of the most tragic times of my life and I want to dedicate it to the two people whose love inspired me forward.

First, my incredibly compassionate, brilliant and talented teenage daughter who faces the challenges, along with her peers, of the modern-day experience pulling them away from connection to the very source of personal freedom.

Ethne, may your brilliance shine a light into the future and thank you for your love, support and contribution of the two sonnets in the book. Wonderland, written Dec 2017, inspired by the "Splintered" book series, author A. G. Howard and This Place, written Dec 2017

Secondly, Rodolfo, a very special man of honor and valor who loves me enough to hold my precious wings through my darkest hour. My deepest gratitude to you for witnessing my humanity, messiness, vulnerability and inspiring me through yours.

My Gratitude

I wanted to write this book and my story because I wanted to offer hope and inspiration and it will soon be obvious that I am not the sole provider of that, I am but a sliver of the power, inspiration and rawness which lays between these pages.

When I asked my coaches to write about their journeys to contribute to the book I had a plan of how the book was going to go. I decided however to not write the parts I was responsible for until I read their chapters, and I am so glad I waited. It changed everything.

I am so blessed these amazing women were willing to share their inner most depths and their successes and failures along the way. To speak to you with open hearts and so intimately. The strength and courage they show and possess is why they were invited to the Evolution Coaching program and it's what makes them the truly unique kickass women and powerhouse coaches they are today.

If you want to lead people into the battle of their lives, their exploration to attain personal freedom, you must be a stellar example of vulnerability and strength. If you want to inspire people to grow and push past their fears you have to understand what you are asking them to do. You have to have applied the process, to have faced the demons, to have fought your way to the place where you were victorious... and you should have failed along the way.

You should have failed because the act of failing and getting back up and going at it again is one of the most insightful and powerful experiences anyone can have. This book is that triumph. It is the intimate journey of four brave and powerful women who took on the challenge to struggle towards attaining personal freedom and to go on to encourage and assist others to do so as well.

Thank you, Bev, Robyn, Keli and Donnaah for your belief in the program and me, for your tenacity to grow and discover yourself and for the gift of contributing your words and stories to this project.

There will be others who come after you, taking on the challenge to becoming members of the most exclusive and highly trained coaches in the world and you will be their inspiration as well. In the end, you all will carry on my legacy and mission, and for that I am eternally grateful.

Thousands of lives will be touched by your stories, minds and hearts will open, hope will bloom, and it will be realized that there is a way out of anxiety, depression, past traumas, addictions, or the self-made prisons many find themselves in.

I know the vulnerability shared here will seed others, will allow them to believe they can indeed heal from the past, to deprogram the falsehoods in their minds and to walk, run, scrape and claw their way to discover and attain their personal freedom.

Bravo to you all!

Contents

PART ONE

This Place

I hear them howl into the dark night
they run through the woods looking like shadows
they are there in the snow, in the moonlight
Here I am looking out the cracked windows

My bike tears along the wooded trailways
I feel as free as a wolf in these woods
the eagles soar free out here at midday
She asked if she could fly, I said she could

We sat there on that mountain top laughing
she told me that she wanted to stay here
we were there cause she loved photographing
I feel so alive with the wind so near

Why can't we ever just stay in one place
I looked at her and saw tears on her face

~Ethne Diamond

The Short Story of Jill

Jill walked in timidly and sat down on the closest piece of furniture she could, she looked truly uncomfortable. I was almost afraid to talk because I thought she would bolt. I took a breath and waited... then I took some more. I realized I shouldn't talk and neither should she... she had been talking way too much about her issues. She needed to feel.

It took seven of the longest minutes of silence before she started crying. I kept breathing and quiet. Five minutes of soft crying led to six minutes of real deep sobbing, gut wrenching heaves and lots of snot. I motioned to the Kleenex.

Another three minutes of hiccup crying, and Jill then became quiet and looked up to meet my eyes. I smiled and we both started laughing. We laughed so hard we both ended up heading to the bathroom at the same time which made us laugh some more.

I let Jill go first and when I came back out she was sitting upright beside my chair, eyes wide and clear and she was smiling. I sat down and said, "ok, let's get started".

Jill told me about the sexual abuse she had suffered as a child at the hands of her father, brother and grandfather. She told me of the emotional and sexual abuse of her first boyfriend, and the second boyfriend and then her life being forced into sex work until she was 24. She said she felt beyond broken and just wanted to die, I was her last effort, after years of trying everything. She said she wanted to let go of the past, be free from the things that had happened.

At this point I interrupted her and said, "Let's stop all this story shall we, including the I want to die stuff." Jill looked a little stunned. I said "this isn't talk therapy, I don't want to focus on your past other than to understand how your past programming has led to your current strategies, and most importantly where you want to go NOW. Also, you can't let go of the past or be free from what happened, it's all part of you. What you want to do is integrate it and deprogram the triggers. You really want to get current."

Did that seem rude to you, that I interrupted her story, that I didn't let her go on about her past, that I told her that her wanting to die was not the important part? It wasn't rude, it was in fact lifesaving. It's called a pattern interrupt.

The reality is talking about your stuff doesn't change it, it just teaches you to feel comfortable talking about it. If anything, it solidifies your story and programming even deeper into your subconscious. It can make you feel better for a while and it doesn't lead to long term change. It leads to resignation or feeling like a survivor, both mean the core patterns are still there.

Many self-help techniques, modalities and tools teach you to cope with, or distract, or disconnect from, to dampen down the emotions, some even teach you to try to control your emotional landscape. None of that is actually leading you to your personal freedom.

Wanting to change doesn't help you change it just leaves you feeling defeated if you don't have a plan to follow that is successful. Workshops that leave you feeling all high and awesome don't lead to sustainable long-term changes because they are creating high dopamine levels in your brain and then you feel the letdown coming back to 'real' life.

Trying to do it yourself typically doesn't create the changes you need because you aren't a good judge of what's BS and past programming and not. Nor is your intuition going to work either because any type of past abuse, neglect or anxiety as a child has damaged that mechanism and until you deprogram your past it stays broken.

I don't mean to make everything sound doom and gloom... because there are solutions and you can heal, even from such trauma as the client Jill in the above story. However, it is going to take some time. It probably won't take five years, or ten, not even three for most of the people I have worked with once they have the right plan.

After our work Jill was integrated and healthy within two years, pretty fast for someone who had suffered for over 35 years and had tried everything she knew was available. And 15 years later she is still rock solid and going beyond anything she thought was ever possible for her. She is physically healthy, spiritually healthy, emotional healthy, no more anxiety and depression or thoughts of suicide. Jill loves with her husband and is enjoying fabulous sex (she never thought that was possible) and she created a healthy bond with their child. She is also thrilled about her job. No more self-help, therapy, or workshops to take. She just does a few 5 minute practices daily and that's it. Jill is personal free from any past programs that don't work for her and her current strategies enable her amazing life.

There are truly only two things holding you back from everything you want to heal or desire to achieve and living in your personal freedom. Two things; your past programming and your current strategies. Pretty simple really. There are only two very simple thing you need to do to change that. Stop doing what you don't want to do and get present and inhabit your body fully. Easy, right? It is. However, people typically need a lot more than just "knowing" this.

Realizing that we needed more than just understanding this intellectually I created a rock-solid kick ass program to deliver the rest of the secret sauce, the other pieces of the puzzle. A multi-dimensional program that goes to work somatically, sub-consciously, biochemically, energetically, emotionally and all the ways you require to create permanent change. I have everything lined up for you, everything except the action and courage, those are up to you.

Instead of writing a dry book about how it all works... I am going to give you an overview in Part One and then my coaches and I are going to let you in behind the scenes to the real juice. Let you see how this all shakes out when it involves real people doing the real work to attain their personal freedom.

Each coach's chapter was written by them, in their voice in their style, mostly unedited so we get the reality and rawness of their process. I think you'll love how their uniqueness and personalities come alive through the pages. This is the powerful intimate and courageous journey of growth and healing of my first four Evolution Coaches and a little of my journey of the creation of the High Speed Evolution program.

Grab a box of tissues, a beverage and snack, get comfy because I believe you won't want to put this book down for even one second.

Personal Freedom

Before we dive into the coach's stories in part two of the book I did wish to give you some background and foundation of understanding to better appreciate the path these wonderful women embarked upon. There are some terms and definitions that will assist you as well and a little piece of the why and how this all started. To me, living a life of Personal Freedom is paramount and as you read these pages you will see why.

Personal Freedom, as defined by the High Speed Evolution program, is being fully resourced and fully integrated, living your Peak Experience.

Peak Experience of course is different for all of us, depending on the goals and lifestyles we live and desire to live. One person might desire to live on a beach and have a family, spending time with family as their most important value and need. Others might want to conquer the world of surfing or spend a life in a monastery. Before we even know, we have to become truly self-aware to be able design our lives purposefully.

It's incredibly important to design your life purposefully, with the understanding as you grow you will be course correcting. Looking towards your desires and the dreams you want to create is fuel for a purposeful and satisfying life well lived.

When you attain Personal Freedom, you have mastery over your inner life and outer life, outer life to the extent possible, meaning the things you actually have control over. You aren't waiting for outside forces to exert pressure forcing your changes, you have the ability to navigate change and personal evolution from within, rapidly, consistently, sustainably any time you choose.

You have trained yourself to be master of your biochemistry and your subconscious mind. You have access to your deepest authentic knowing, your body wisdom and your deepest guided intuition.

You have learned to let go of being responsible for others and moved into supporting them, you stopped assuming and create clear conversations and agreements, you hold flexible boundaries, you are in integrity with yourself and others, accountable for your parts and knowing which ones aren't yours, you're able to navigate your emotional landscape in a full and grounded way. All this means you are solid in your life come what may.

You've got this, even when there are outside forces of chaos in your life which are pretty well guaranteed as long as you are living and loving.

Our Jailer

Everyone desires to be happy and free. Freedom usually comes up on my client's assessment worksheets as something they truly desire and value above or close to love. Why is freedom such an important concept for us when in reality most people will never truly experience it?

Spiritually we could say it's because we long to return to pure energy without the constraints we have as humans in this physical container. Some people believe transcendence or enlightenment is the answer to escape the deep internal discontent. I know though it's way more earth based than that.

At the very essence of our being we know we are trapped by something. From the gravity that keeps us from flying off the earth, to the clock that keeps on ticking reminding us minute to minute that our time is finite. Truth be told we are imprisoned, and by things more covert than the time we have on the planet. We're trapped by our internal patterns that are programmed into us by our influencers such as our parents and society. We're trapped by our own evolutionary survival mechanisms meant to keep us safe which are backfiring in the world we currently inhabit.

So, we search for freedom without even knowing where it is we're confined. We may think money is the problem, so we make money to buy us things and take us places, to experience what we believe might be that elusive feeling...freedom. The freedom of wealth and time. Yet once we're there we still feel restless, because there is nothing external that will actually relieve us.

Perhaps then we think we are really looking for enlightenment or transcendence, a freedom from stress, anger or worry, from the everyday complexities of life. We declutter, simplify, minimize, Feng Shui, meditate, do yoga, fast, go on visions quests and sometimes leave all material and worldly attachments behind.

And once again, in our depths we still feel it... the grip inside, the 'knowing' we aren't really free. We don't get that our struggle is futile because we don't understand the very mechanisms at work, and we will either finally give up and become apathetic or we will carry on carrying on, searching... but rarely finding a sustainable experience or answer.

Our true captor is the internal directive of our inner most primal mechanisms, and while they play an incredibly important role, to save us from pain, death, keep us safe, streamline our internal process so we can react and automate, our modern lifestyle has created a misalignment. In this modern era our primal directives can hinder us and paralyze our minds, emotions and keep us from feeling free and ultimately at peace.

These internal mechanisms and programs were an essential part of our survival in the not too distant past, now our experiences have changed drastically, and we have not evolved our primary survival functions fast enough to accommodate those changes. Our survival mechanisms are now our prisons, the programming that was designed to keep us safe, now keeps us stuck and unhappy, and makes attaining true long-lasting change tough.

Understanding we are stuck IN ourselves gives us the key to understand the power to get out of the cage is within ourselves as well. I like to call it The Art of Insourcing.

To feel personally free, one must be able to make sustainable changes easily and reliably, to have healed and integrated past traumas, be able to be present, current and have access to the full wisdom of one's body and not just one's mind.

Next, I want to share my personal journey that started me on the path of attaining personal freedom.

Pulling the Trigger— My Journey

I want to share with you a small part of my road to personal freedom, so you might have a tad more understanding about why creating High Speed Evolution became and is still my mission in my life.

I had a pretty rough go of it in my early life, rape, childhood sexual abuse, physical violence, neglect, alcoholic Dad, chemically unbalanced Mom, emotional abuse and some serious injuries. By the time I was in my late teens I had suffered a nervous breakdown and went into a self-destruct spiral.

I had in essence been programmed and patterned; biologically created for self-sabotage, isolation, disconnection, depression and hopelessness. Entering into adulthood I was in the thick of those directives and I succumbed to the neurochemical changes made by it all.

It all ended (or started depending on your perspective) with me on my knees in a field at sunrise, with a loaded gun to my head, pulling the trigger. At the moment, the hammer hit I had a revelation of sorts. I don't know if it was God or the Universe or my Tantra Master to be, who had my back that morning however I received a profound awakening and answers to the questions I had asked in life.

Why me? Why is it so hard to let go of pain? Why is it so tough to be open and vulnerable? Why do people hurt each other? How do I trust? How do I embrace life fully when everything is so scary? Why do I do self-destructive things? Why is change so hard?

When I pulled the trigger and the hammer hit, the vibration started at my temple and rushed down my spine to my tailbone. I gasped as a rush of white searing hot pain shot up my spine and blew my head open (thankfully not literally). My physical body felt as though it split open down the middle, my container coming completely apart. I cried out loud, all my breath leaving my body, completely emptying me of everything. No sound, no motion, no thought, no breath, nothing. Nothing...

And then as though time restarted and unfolded in my cells, I gasped and inhaled forcefully as though it were my first breath ever and I felt the universe pour in through my open skull. There are no words to actually describe the experience and in all these years I have tried a few times, only to fail miserably. I know I won't succeed here either truthfully, so I'll keep it short. You can ask me about it sometime if you wish.

I wasn't able to take in the immensity of what I was experiencing. I thought I had died. I had no body sensations at all. It was as though I had evaporated. I lay in the field, in the grass, staring at the sun. After what seemed like a lifetime, came an immense feeling, gratitude coursing through me, though at the time I wouldn't have recognized that's what it was.

I "woke" up ALIVE! Alive in a way that I'd never known. Vibrating in exquisite euphoria. Seeing new colors and hearing new sounds, experiencing feelings in my body I couldn't comprehend. It was clear something drastic had happened. I huddled in a ball to quiet the overwhelm. I had gone mad, I was sure of it. I was positive that if I were alive the bullet had caused severe brain damage.

Finally, I stood up and I felt superhuman, and I experienced an existential crisis in reverse. I understood that the code to change was imbedded in us and if we hacked our deepest built in primal defense mechanism we could unleash our FULL human potential and create sustainable deep transformation at any level. I felt this at every level of my being. I "knew" this fully.

After that my life changed drastically, altered radically. I was attaining personal freedom, the ability to make easy, sustainable change from within not waiting for external forces to create the impetus. I was unlocking parts of my evolutionary design and rearranging them. I had found answers and understanding of how we were suffering as a species by not being able to evolve at the speed we were advancing technologically. How we were needlessly trapped and dying because we didn't know how to make the changes from internal will versus waiting for external forces to make things unbearable.

Although the events of that day had an immediate effect on me and I was radically altered I still wanted to be completely protected against new trauma and the chaos that happens in a big life. I need a plan to make sure I and anyone I was going to teach this new paradigm of "Mastery In Your Being" to was going to be bulletproof LOL. No pun intended.

I spent the next fifteen years, researching and formulating the processes to unlock more of the bounds of human limits and potential. I apprenticed in Ancient wisdom and secrets, I worked with incredibly intense art forms that defied the beliefs of many, even myself. I learned from healers, shamans, and nature all over the world. I studied "real" sciences, psychology, anatomy, modern brain science as well as alternative therapies, naturopathic modalities, peak performance, NLP, hypnotherapy, and just about anything I could get my hands on.

I was understanding and gathering knowledge and experience at an accelerated pace as I had the advantage of several innate gifts as well the skills I gained in my "death revelation". I can't take credit for the ones hardwired in from birth, a high IQ, an eidetic memory and the ability to read over 2000 words a minute. Actually, it's less like reading and more like taking pictures of whole pages anyway, these all served me well in my quest.

The practices of High Speed Evolution and the Art of Insourcing, were finally birthed and after mastering them myself I started working with others, experimenting and refining. They have proven 99 percent successful with everyone who has ever done them. The full story is for another time and another book. I just wanted you to have some background as you move forward here with us.

Next up let's explore a bit about why change can be so hard and what to do about that.

Larry, the Baby Osprey

Change was designed to be hard, it's necessary that it be hard, because the more we can do without thinking about things the more we keep our brain's resources freed up and on the ready for things that might need our attention, like dangerous circumstances. We shouldn't have to think about getting dressed, how to drive, walk, eat and all the thousands of things we do daily. Therefore, the brain lays down pathways like super highways for the things we do over and over again, it creates our internal programs and patterns, our habits. It automates us.

Once these super highways are laid down, the brain resists changing them because it takes a tremendous effort to break through and make new connections, especially if something was laid down in the earlier years of our lives. From an evolutionary stand point the patterns we lay down in our younger years are for survival purposes, to help keep us alive. At least that's how it was, and this is where some of the problems we are experiencing now take place.

Evolutionarily, a major change is created by extreme forces pushing against our patterns on either end of a spectrum. It can be an external slow-moving process over generations, like losing a food source or climate change. Or it can happen through a huge external fast acting force, like an earthquake or flood. Both are external forces, and both can interrupt deep patterns within us, though we will strive to seek homeostasis as soon as we can, IF we can.

This shows us that change is natural and essential, it's part of our process and yet for many people it's so incredibly frustrating and short lived when trying to make changes from WITHIN without the external forces at play. Most people do what's natural, wait for things to get painful or too unbearable before they are able to bring to bear the change they need and want. We are even taught in marketing DON'T use the word change, no one wants to hear that.

Ok, so what's the benefit of being hardwired or programmed if it gives us so much grief. Let's look to a real life natural scenario to examine the purpose of hardwiring pathways which resist change.

At the time of this writing I live on a beautiful island in the PNW and there are a mated pair of Osprey that fish off our beach. Osprey are one of the most successful fish hunters in the bird of prey world and have a unique way of flying with their catch. Osprey's front toes are opposable, like our thumbs and they can rotate backward, so after the Osprey catches their fish, they turn the fish head first so it's easier to fly with. That's cool and yet the amazing story is when the Osprey start to teach their babies how to survive.

Imagine if you will that you are Larry, a baby Osprey in a nest. All you know is food comes from your mama. You are hungry, and she feeds you. Now it won't be long, just 51 - 54 days before you will start flying. Once that happens it's important you start to understand where food really comes from.

Your young brain is laying down electrical pathways, these neural pathways are what you will rely on to know what to do.

Your job is to model and learn, by observation and association, how to get along in the world and it's your Osprey parents job to make sure they teach you how to do so.

First safety is in the nest under your parents, then your parents start to spend time at the sides of the nest leaving you vulnerable. You cry and let them know you are unhappy and scared. They come to you and then leave again. They know you have to be uncomfortable if you are going to make the leaps to the changes coming ahead.

Still food comes to you at the nest from your parent until one day, your mom flies by you with the food dangling from her feet. You cry out hungry and she flies by again. You plead with her and yet she persists until you move to the side of the nest, hunger driving you past your fear. She then feeds you and settles in with you and you are happy.

The next day she flies by again and again and each day it's longer until she feeds you. Each day you get more desperate until one day you fly after her trying to get the fish. She flies back to the nest with you following and feeds you.

I can hear this part going on as the babies cry and cry all day long. I think about how hard the work is to teach the baby to have to make the huge psychological leap from food coming from parents to fishing for himself, and it has to happen fast. Within the time of that first flight to hunting on their own is about two to three weeks and it's a hard time for the babies and parents.

Imagine there you are watching your parent bring you food and take it father away each day and feeding you later and later each day. You fly after your Dad and he takes you over water. One day he drops the precious fish he was dangling behind him enticing you to follow. You watch, and he dives down to get it before it hits the water. Soon he lets it hit the water and a little while after that you are actually following him, watching the whole process as he hunts for your food.

Then the lightbulb goes on! Food comes from the water and I hunt it when I am hungry. Now you go out and hone your skills of survival day after day. If you are fortunate you're a good hunter like your parents and you survive to migrate several thousand miles that winter to never see your family again.

So why this story? Well you did the same thing as a baby, child and teen. You emulated what your parents showed you and what they told you. For survival sake, you laid down deep trenches of information in your brain, in your cells and in your bio chemistry, the information that you needed to survive. The problem is... we don't live the way we evolved to live. We don't live "natural" lives now therefore these primal mechanisms are really messing with us in a bad way. The patterns and programs laid down by our caregivers have little to do with survival today and real dangers and more to do with dysfunctions, fears, and bad habits passed on through the generations.

Our path is no longer a simple matter of learning basic survival skills and the need to be steadfast and not easily changeable. Flexibility is needed for flourishing and thriving and in fact it is the new paradigm of our evolution. Hop on board or become extinct. Let's examine what's going wrong with our natural process that has served us well until the last 100 years or so.

The Flaw in Our Evolutionary Design

The dictionary states one of the definitions of evolution, as (Biology) change in the gene pool of a population from generation to generation by such processes as mutation, natural selection, and genetic drift.

How does evolution/internal change happen? I'll give you a simple explanation for our purposes, and any evolution expert give me some latitude here ok?

Evolution is created by outside forces/changes exerting pressure or pressures on a thing causing the thing to change or become extinct. Change or die, it's a pretty big deal.

Evolution is natural and needed, however when it comes to humans living in the world currently, ours is wreaking havoc on many of us. The external forces being applied to us are beyond what we can adapt to fast enough and quite frankly we are dying a slow tortuous death as a species because of it.

Pretty well since the invention of the light bulb we've had external forces pushing upon us faster than we can keep up with and we are just sinking deeper into internal conflict. Our lifestyles and technological advances are taking us further away from our natural state and compromising us deeply.

We're suffering from the lack of connection of grounding into the earth, spending time outside seeing, hearing and breathing REAL life. A lack of appropriate sleep timing, not just eight hours but the WHEN of sleep, being in bed before 10pm. We don't do enough physical motion or too much of the wrong kind, we eat fake food, we use too much technology, we become disconnected from ourselves and others though artificially high levels of dopamine and not enough oxytocin and real connection, we have lost true intimacy... we are drowning in overwhelm, anxiety and decision fatigue.

Anxiety is a byproduct of this disconnection that is happening to us. The higher up we live in our energy system making our heads full and leaving our bodies in the dust, the more we fail to thrive. Anxiety is so prevalent, such a modern normal state, most people don't even recognize they are living in it.

The flip side of anxiety is depression. I believe depression is the body's natural way of attempting to save us because we can't live in a state of high anxiety all the time. It is truly scary how many people are suffering from this diagnosis and are being medicated with drugs which will change their natural ability to regulate their own chemistry and leave them with a serious chemical imbalance for good. Especially since all we need to do to get rid of depression symptoms is to deal with the underlying anxiety. Decades of working with people who are depressed has proven this to me.

This all means is we're allowing external forces to push us away from our very life blood, the very things which have enabled us to survive and thrive for thousands of years and instead we are replacing those enriching connecting needed lifelines with diseased lifestyles. We're replacing our true happiness with pseudo-happiness, we're wiring our brains for higher and higher needs of dopamine hits and leaving the true life sustaining benefits of oxytocin behind.

Ok, so understanding we are on a crash course isn't enough to make us veer from that path because we are here due to the very way evolution designed our brains. We're designed to STAY the course once the program was laid down in our brain's neural pathways and chemistry. We are created to stick to our programming at all costs because this is where safety is thought to reside, this is what we were designed to do. Yet, now we need to let go of hanging on because it's putting us in danger, not saving us from it.

We desperately need to reverse parts of this evolutionary process by making a few tweaks, undoing the old programming and laying down a new set of pathways which enable us to make changes easily, sustainable and quickly from the inside out. Training our bodies and brains to be efficient and easily flexible to our internal will.

I believe it's imperative to be in conscious charge of breaking old internal paradigms and replacing them with ones that will enhance your life, your health, your relationships, your financial picture, and enable you to live life by your true values and needs.

Let's take a look at what happens on the precipice of change and why we tend to pull away and sabotage ourselves right before we break through.

Set on Self Sabotage

Let's say you decide you want to be a morning workout person, you know working out is good for you and you can't seem to get to the gym after work and you heard the morning is better anyway. You decide Monday morning is the day you will create the change. Why Monday? Who knows but we tend to think we can make changes more easily along with significant time experiences, like Mondays as the start of the week, or mornings as the start of the day, or New Year's as the start of the year. It isn't true but, yet we think this way.

The first morning, you manage to drag yourself up and out and get to the gym all the while grumbling you are not a morning person. Day 2 you succeed. Day 3 good to go. Day 4 you feel like a rock start and it's true we tend to lean towards things that make us feel good and success does that.

Now getting up in the morning is requiring will power and that's actually a finite resource. The more you have to use it the less you have to use, which is why we typically do better with things we use will power for in the morning because by late afternoon or evening we have run out of it and succumb.

After a period of time of achieving getting up and working out, and this timing can be different for everyone and you have your very own pattern around it, your brain starts to realize this might be a permanent change and not just a temporary" crisis". Because it takes tremendous resources to construct a new neural pathway, a new "you are a morning workout person" model the brain doesn't want to go there if it doesn't have to. Remember these original brain programs were built to keep you "safe" (even if this isn't true) so the brain sees no good reason to change the way you are.

When your brain realizes you are serious about this new pattern and it's going to have to "change" but before it makes this a permanent new directive, it takes one last major effort to thwart you. Your subconscious mind which has no judgement to understand that this new pattern is healthy, rebels to keep everything the same. It does this by releasing chemicals, somatic experiences and "thoughts" to alert and try to convince you that you're in danger.

Day 12 you wake up and feel like you are run down, you were raised to believe if you feel even a little bit sick you should rest and stay home. You hear yourself say, get up, time to work out and yet there is that part of you that says, NO, I'm sick, I need rest. I'll get back to it tomorrow, and you turn over and sleep that extra hour before work.

Now you might be saying, "Tanja are you trying to tell me my subconscious mind created an illness to keep from making the change permanent?" Why yes, I am saying exactly that.

In my programs, I can tell when someone is ready to make a huge permanent shift because they go a little crazy. They either get really ill, or start having some other physical issue, or they start to believe following me is dangerous and I am leading them to an unsound experience or any numerous of odd, confused and unbalanced thinking.

Confusion is a clear sign of impending pattern change because it takes a bit, I believe 24-48 hours (once the new routine has been going on for a while) for the brain to move from one mode of automation to another. It's like updating your device. Once that happens it is important to continue to go down that path consistently for a bit longer to solidify the new pathways and create sustainable permeant pattern changed.

There's also a very real scary thing that can happen when big core patterns are about to be replaced and I'll tell you all about that next.

By the way, the 21 days to a new habit was based on a study in a controlled environment where they guys wore upside down googles 24/7 and it took their brains 21 days to create a new shift. So, if you have tried to change a habit and did something for 21 days and then failed to make it stick, don't worry you didn't fail, first you didn't do it 24/7 and it takes more than JUST doing something for 21 days if it is a big shift.

At the Edge of The Void

There's this phenomenon which happens when you create a new neural pathway from a very old and entrenched program or a network of them. I call it experiencing the Edge of the Void, or as Bev, one of the coaches has said, the edge of your personal unknown.

You won't feel this as much with smaller neural pathways changes, but the ones which have big networks, fibers that weave around the very fabric of who you believe you are, then yes, most definitely this will happen.

The void is place many people who are on a self-growth path step up to and then turn back and run to safety from, sometimes only once but more often than not, over and over again. This experience is the one which leaves people believing they can't change or believing they need a different self-help program or different workshop, etc.

The reason big core change can be so scary is because once you create the process of deprogramming, when the destruction of one pathway occurs as another is being built, there is nothing in front of you to take its place. As you stand looking into the void it feels like facing death, and truthfully it is. It is the demise of an old and familiar path created in your brain by your past and the death of who you believe you are and were.

It's the most lonely and courageous adventure you will ever face. To stand, staring into the void, the unknown self, and walk forward CREATING your path as you go. Yet it's the only way YOUR authentic truth is created AND the only way YOUR Personal Freedom will be attained.

Just like all growth and healing, moving into the void takes place in the spaces between the action. It occurs in the stillness of the moment. That pause between the breath, the space between the atoms, and as you take the next in breath, inspiration fills you and becomes the expression of your presence in each next moment, moving you forward letting go of old programs and experiencing the creation of you authentically.

It's beyond all reasonable survival instincts and an assault to everything primal in you, to step into the void. Our prime directive of survival is habitually on high alert about these immense pattern interrupts. Remember the internal prime directive is to stay the course unless an outside extreme experience forces you to change.

Thousands of cultures have centuries upon centuries of traditions surrounding these breakthroughs, all of them guided by elders, mentors, shamans, or others who have walked into their own unknown. We need someone to guide us when we reach the void. We need support to stay the course to know we are on the right track as it's not intuitive, it's not logical, it's not "natural" to walk out into "nothingness".

Some cultures create induced experiences which gives one the feeling of having created new pathways but rarely does this actually happen permanently. The same happens with most workshops that get your dopamine levels going. You get these amazing feelings and epiphanies and then once you're back home... nothing sticks. This can lead you to a self-help or workshop "addiction", where you keep seeking out the feeling of change and the chemistry "feeling" of the revelation and connection and yet not really get there permanently.

The Edge of the Void is an intense place and yet it's also the place where your ultimate freedom comes from. Once you become familiar with your void and have walked beyond it several times you will have what I call Mastery in Your Being, and will be able to create pattern restructuring with so much ease it feels like magic.

You might be wondering what are the practices, technologies and support one needs to make all this happen more effectively and without personal trial and error. The coaches have written about some of the processes they went through in the next part of the book. I will fill you in with an overview in just a moment.

High Speed Evolution

High Speed Evolution- is the most powerful and unique personal development program in the world. It took me 15 years to create it. Not because it's complicated but actually because of its fantastic and utter simplicity.

I created it to be easy to understand and implement, be user friendly to all belief systems and genders, fit into a busy lifestyle, be sustainable, get crazy awesome results, integrate into all the body systems (subconscious mind, logical mind, cellular memories, energetics), fly under the radar of the amygdala (our internal alarm system) and to allow you to hack your natural inclination to wait for outside forces as the impetus to change. Whew. No easy feat.

Oh and it had to work for everyone and on every challenge, be the lynch pin of the core of our issues. I eventually succeeded, after thousands of hours of experimenting on myself and then others, and endlessly refining each step.

HSE works, some say like magic. But it isn't magic it's a very simple to do but supremely complex technology that evolves as you do, it is dynamic and alive. HSE is my core program taught in two ways. High Speed Evolution private one on one, or the Your Personal Evolution group coaching program.

HSE - The Five Evolutions to Life Mastery, one on one is taught at the pace of the individual and is typically between a twelve and eighteen-month experience.

Your Personal Evolution is taught as an online group program with each evolution being six month. Each Evolution is complete in itself though a high percentage of people who start the program go on to complete all Five of the Evolutions. There are then a select few invited to the Evolution Coach Training Program, to be certified to coach others in the HSE practices.

There was an evolution to the name and structure of the HSE program through the first couple of years, so you might see references to that while reading the coaches stories. Although I had been teaching these practices to thousands of people over the years before the group program, I had never had a name for them and doing mostly one on one coaching through referrals I didn't really need one.

When I first decided to do a group coaching program back in January of 2014 I decided to do it for 6 months and around the study of Tantra, using the HSE micro-practices, so I called it a six-month Tantra Group coaching program and it was such a hit the group made me extend it to nine months.

I had just finished writing the book Riding The Phoenix that summer about my early life and how the practices were created so I decided to rename the group coaching program in the fall of 2014 when I started Level Two and another level One, to Riding The Phoenix group coaching.

As things progressed and the group coaching program continued to be popular and creating amazing successes for the students I realized this was here to stay and I scrambled to Evolve the program into a full personal development program like the one I had been using for my high end one on one coaching clients in my Inner Circle. So, Your Personal Evolution group coaching was born from my High Speed Evolution-the Five Evolutions to Life Mastery course and I also created a Certified Coaching program while I was at it.

Evolution One- Your Life Unleashed - (you may find references to me lovingly calling it, Your Personal Hell by the coaches, because it can be tough to discover your life has not really been your own)

Evolution Two- Your Personal Freedom

Evolution Three - Your Impassioned Truth

Evolution Four- Your Awakened Passion and Purpose

Evolution Five- Your Courageous Action

Like all of life, flexibility is a key component when in the mix of it all and rising to the occasion to create is the process of evolution, and my life is no different. Today the group program is steady and solidly loving its place in the world. No more name or structure changes. Whew.

In the preceding pages you learned about how we are designed to "stay the course" laid out for us in our youth, you learned why change can be tough and how you can want to change something and still not get there or get there permanently. You learned about the self-sabotage mechanisms at work when you are on the brink of a big breakthrough and the scariest part, The Edge of The Void.

In the next chapters you will have a front row seat to the power of change and the intimate experiences of my first four certified coaches as they implemented the practices that transformed their lives forever.

These four amazing women share their stories of breakthroughs and challenges, fears and courage on the edge of the Void. I trust you will see yourself in one or a couple of them, will feel their experiences and at the end applaud their journeys as I have.

Please note that they continue to grow and flourish past the completion of the program and their coach training and they have incredible successes with their clients as well. Ok let's get to it.

PART TWO

Wonderland

We float on the ocean made up of tears
in this wooden rowboat, him beside me
moths in his room fluttered behind mirrors
drunk on the berries, I won't leave him be

Dancing on the sun I was at last free
my heart was split in two, who would I choose
why can't I always be free, just be me
looked and shouted, what do I have to lose

You're sobbing for him, yet you bled for me
I wish I could just fly away from this
He whispered that it was all up to me
my dark angel leaned in for one last kiss

Standing in the stars I was at last free
I embraced the thought that I was just me

~Ethne Diamond

The Coaches

Ridiculous Life, Glorious Mess

Becoming undone in just the right way

Donnaah Sparkle

Donnaah

I've been training to be a coach my entire life. Or rather, my entire life has been a training ground for moving me towards life coaching and life mastery. Or rather I was born to be a Soul guide and purpose illuminator and have been re-remembering and growing into that gift for my whole life. Until now. Because now I am joyfully occupying the just right space of my purpose intersecting with my passion, shored up by my own personal sense of integrity, as I go about my amazingly courageous life.

As a child, I used to dream that I was mediating between the Devil and God. I stood in the middle of the heavens and screamed and bargained and danced and negotiated in some magical fashion between the forces of Good and Evil. Except now I know there are no such forces, per se, no such things as Good or Evil. The world isn't polarity; it is flow. And still I stand, a pillar, between Heaven and Earth and I scream and bargain and dance and negotiate. It's no longer a dream but a real, raw, courageous life where I know I am everything and I am nothing.

So many experiences, so many successes and failures, so much pain, immense pleasure, opportunities lost, amazingness manifested. All of it. All of me. My own little corner of the world where I serve and laugh, and my hearts sings and shines. I've created it and it's mine.

Most people in our culture have no idea what I am talking about. To live a quiet life of integrity and freedom really isn't very lofty or sexy. It's not worth a second look because in our culture, everything is such a BFD now. Drama and hyperbole and "all about me" rules. Everything must be recorded, photographed, exclaimed upon, commented about, Facebook liked. This is how we are seduced into living our lives by this world's standards, exterior to us, influenced by vast expectations that are external to our inner experiences and truth.

But there is another way to live without the need to be validated every step of the way.

There is a radical way to learn to live, without the need for others to continually support and understand and applaud our every step (as long as it makes sense to them). This other way of living, an orientation really, is called insourcing. Insourcing is part awareness, part trust, part listening, part not giving a damn, and part courage. Once I learned to source and be resourced from within, I was able to create a clear vision of what I wanted and then let it come to me in divine timing.

Ultimate self-trust and trust in the way of how it is takes courage and deep relaxation in the body. And this leads to ultimate freedom of being who I am, how I am, in the present moment, led by Spirit and my own knowing, being in integrity with myself first and foremost and last and lastmost.

For me, freedom arises from being in deep personal, spiritual, and emotional integrity and having multidimensional awareness of the malleable and changeable truth of the present moment iteration of me. It is acting in accordance with what is real for me in any moment. And allowing the present moment to inform what is true for me, to inform what is next for me, to inform me of how it is with me. A self-perpetuating cycle of input, listening, discernment, action.

And Integrity. When I am living in integrity, it's like life has pulled out all the stops and triggers and given me the keys to my kingdom. I have undeniable self-knowledge of what is mine and what is not mine, what belongs and what doesn't belong with me on my journey. Integrity is divine bliss and steadfast vision. It pulls out all the stops and drops me headfirst into trust and knowing and deep listening to what is, not to all the things I used to listen to, the shouldas, couldas, wouldas, might have beens.

So, how did I come to understand and embody insourcing, which is really an expansive and in-depth self-awareness? How did I come to live in integrity? Ah, well, for me, first I had to recognize when I was out of integrity to then begin to know how to live in accordance with my own sense of integrity.

As I moved through this journey, I came to recognize that tension, stress, looping thoughts, irritation, doubt, and lack of self-confidence are signals to me that I am out of integrity in some area of my life. First, I have to be willing to feel all the things, feel the tension and irritation and doubt without getting so walloped by my feelings that I can't feel through them to the truth of what is out of alignment.

When I am in alignment with where I am going and how I am being, I am willing to look like a slacker, a loser, and a misfit. I know now that I must always put on my own oxygen mask first, so to speak, and be willing to be seen as selfish, wacky, and undutiful. I am willing to look like a total mess as long as I feel I am in integrity with myself.

Before I get into the story of how I came to the Your Personal Evolution program and ultimately a High Speed Evolution coach, I want to state this: I am not here to inspire you, to be interesting or fascinating. My journey through this work and my life isn't a spectator sport for others. I don't want your rah-rahs. I don't want to be a model of inspiration. I don't want to impress you with my journey if you truly aren't willing to change. I'd rather you just scroll on past me and my heartbrokenness, my AHAs, my soul-full expressions. Keep on scrolling past this chapter. I will not give my life away so freely.

This ME has been battled and courageously fought for. Maybe you get it. Maybe you don't get it. But some do, and some will and those are my peeps. The ones who are in the trenches and are living the freakzoid life of expansion and integrity, true grit and passion and emptiness and learning.

I have always known these things that I spent 3 years working with Tanja on. I was just reminding myself of the knowing again. I have spent a decade remembering what I knew: this book contains just a fraction of my most recent journey. This is my information, not yours. I share it with you with compassion and fierceness, a little begrudgingly, to be honest.

Thing is, each of us has and can re-learn the depths of knowing that I express below. But most do not listen to what we know, to what is calling us. We don't listen until we can no longer tolerate not listening, when our cells and dreams bursting with agony over the walls of silence we've put up to block our knowing. It's a raucous, sibilant chorus within, if only we learn to listen.

All the daydreams, the night dreams, the intuitions, the insights, the downloads, the wonderings, the impulses…these are our clues. All the patterns and strategies and mistaken values and needs and expectations of others…these are our undoings. As we become aware of them, we become undone in the just right way to become who we were really meant to be, who our soul dreamed us to be as we were birthed into this life. If we can undo enough of who we have been, we can become who we are here to be.

Who was I when the email about this program showed up in my inbox? I was a lifelong learner, with a MA in Cultural Anthropology and Research Methodology. I had worked for many years as a highly-skilled Research Interviewer for drug and alcohol research projects. Then, I transitioned into Software Quality Assurance, with professional certificates in Software Testing, Technical Writing, and Gerontology.

Smart and curious, I kept feeling my soul being sucked dry trying to live a life that didn't let me sparkle, a life that wasn't authentically me. I was angry, bored, stuck, and depressed. I reached in all directions for programs, teachers, belief systems, anything that felt like change. I had a concept of, but not a devoted practice with, living my life listening to the deep wisdom of my unique essence and following the threads of my soul and purpose.

When this course began, I was already years into my own personal odyssey that had led me to all manner of incredibly interesting, difficult, joyous, unexpected, and just dang extraordinary experiences thus far. This next leg of my journey was gonna be a doozy. But I didn't know it yet.

I had done so many programs. I had already completed 2 coaching certifications and was actively working as a life coach and had a great job in software QA. I was married, not particularly in love, but living a stellar and spectacular lifestyle of outdoor adventures, devoted athleticism, international travel, home restoration projects, creative gardening, gourmet cooking, fabulous cocktails, lots and lots of hiking. So maybe the lack of romance wasn't so important...in any case, I thought I was pretty slick, all embodied and aware and expanded.

After all, I was an energy healer, a Reiki master, a supporter of visionary woman, an excellent coach, etc., etc. I sure didn't need another course. In fact, I had just decided to forgo any more courses or workshops or learnings from teachers.

And then this email came in from a wild woman whom I'd met many years previously and had judged to be way too far out for me. Except, now, she wasn't. I thought "She doesn't feel so crazy and wild to me anymore...huh." My body said YES to the class, Learning Tantra. "Well, hadn't I wanted to study Tantra? It WAS a bucket list item." Huh. If only I'd known but of course my soul knew and that is where the YES came from. So, it began, 3 years of group coaching with Tanja Diamond with coaching certification woven in the last year and a half.

During those 3 years, I got divorced, sold the historic house I had restored, left Seattle after 20 years, changed my name, broke a few hundred patterns, and hit the road as a wanderer in my vintage trailer. I pretty much dismantled my whole life, personas, and identities, and gave up anything that looked like plans. I learned to dance with uncertainty and laugh at the unknown.

Along the way, I trained as a High Speed Evolution coach. Now as I trust my Soul and walk with Mystery, my greatest desire in life is to serve others to get unstuck and find true freedom in all areas of their lives so they can step into the kick-ass lives they know they were born to live.

My intention in these few pages is to relate my journey through the 5 evolutions around how my understanding and experience of integrity and life mastery built over the course of

3 years. I focus on my awarenesses and AHAs around my patterns and strategies, specifically in the areas of freedom, courage, integrity, safety, my values, and action taking.

There are more than enough transformation and AHAs in these areas for these few pages and I have deliberately left out my personal explorations and life-altering expeditions in relationship, sexuality, sensuality, and arousal during the 5 levels and beyond. That is for another book because there was such an explosion of permission and knowing in those areas of my life.

So here I was at the start of Evolution 1 and I wrote this about myself as way of introduction:

"I'm 47, 5'7", leanish. Former athlete getting a little soft around the edges by choice, enjoying having a soft belly and strong legs. Dark brown hair dyed red. Dirt always under my ragged fingernails. Lots of hypo pigmentation spots and freckles on my skin. Inevitably wearing something sparkly or pink or other bright colors. Tends towards sensible shoes. A divine, wild, and renegade soul having a super messy human experience. Entranced by imperfect beauty. A fairy butterfly with deep roots in nature and eyes gazing towards the heavens. Relishes home-cooked food and a superb cocktail. Trusting my body's wisdom…most of the time.

My strengths: I get things done, am super organized, can talk with anyone, and have tons of energy (physically, emotionally, and spiritually). I am adventurous, creative, curious, and generally uninterested in others' dramas. I am not afraid to be silly, playful, goofy, and joyful. I express myself along a continuum from silent, powerful presence to crazy antics. I am not afraid to be myself.

My weaknesses: I can be solipsistic, hard-headed, moody, reactionary, fearful, sneaky, manipulative, and passive-aggressive. I tend towards depression when I am not handling my anxiety well. I tend towards a homebody loner when I'm not feeling my power.

My strategies: I tend to play the victim. I use my sadness to put walls up, so I don't have to be vulnerable or intimate. Poor me. I am uncomfortable receiving compliments, yet I crave them hugely, so I angle to get them when I can but then don't want to allow them in. Weird. I am an "open book" and use this to get close to people quickly. I don't hide when I feel truly seen and my authentic wild woman energy can be very attractive to others. I use my smarts as a cover for lack of passion and connection

This is who I thought I was when I began. And in fact, it was me…and it wasn't me. I thought, yeah, I'm pretty self-aware and I've done lots of work and this is just another spiral through self-development. Oh, yes and not exactly and oh my there was so much more than I could have ever in my wildest dreams have conceived or imagined. (This is NOT hyperbole.)

Evolution One
Donnaah

Evolution one, where we began with developing self-awareness and started doing the micro-practices that are so crucial to this work. Or, as Tanja calls this first level: Your Personal Hell.

One of the first assignments was to list my top 6 values. I came up with awe, adventure, beauty, self-love, authenticity, and freedom. These seemed like really good values to want to live life by. Hmmm, but values are more about how I actually was living my life. That said, I think my original values truthfully would have been something like: security, comfort, compromise, fear of judgement, confusion, and denial. These were the energies of how I was actually making decisions in my life. Well, maybe I'm being a little tough on myself. I had an amazing life, by all accounts and witnesses. It's just that much of my life was actually driven by subconscious patterns, cultural conditioning, and childhood strategies.

This is true for most people, even those like myself who had been "doing" personal development for many years, doing all the empowerment workshops, shortcut-to-bliss retreats, and so much training. I was inhabiting my upper chakras and conveniently embracing spiritual bypass to feel like I was doing good work when in fact I was on a treadmill of feeling awesome after a course, workshop, week long training, intensive weekend, and then after coming home, slowly inhabiting the same ol' patterns and making the same ol' choices because what I learned felt good but didn't actually set me up to truly start taking transformative action, to truly start living courageously, or to truly lower my anxiety levels.

This, unbeknownst to me, was no short-cut-to-bliss body of work. Oh, there was to be plenty of bliss. But not without the terror and wild uncertainty of personal evolution. Notice the word Evolution – this means a spiral of development and awareness, not a shortcut to feeling better or good.

I started out employing the usual patterns for me: sorta detached, feeling the group out, holding back from expressing my personal experiences, taking notes during the group calls, experimenting a little with the micro-practices but not really giving it my all. Yep, just like in most every other area of my life, how I did this was how I did most things.

Then, one month in, I began to get that letting go of my patterns was quite a journey. I was able to see them pretty clearly. They'd scream at me, but I'd hold on, then have a moment of total chaos and that would shift me into letting go.

"Argh, it's not pretty over here right now and I am learning to love the mess. I am understanding that the mess is part of the transformation...like, I reach the upper limit of my tolerance of my own crap and finally give in to a new way, a new possibility."

I was beginning to understand how damn hardheaded I was. It would take a cosmic 2x4 to get my full attention sometimes. And even so, I could feel another, more gentle way of being, beyond my patterns, so the letting go was worth it, even as gnarly as it felt.

One month! I hit the ground running, like I usually did because one patterned identity of mine was the go-getter, the A-student, the good girl, the primadonna. I got stuff quickly and I went deep quickly. Going deep is easy enough when you are talking days or weeks, not years. And this was just the first month of what would be end up being 3 years of study. But I didn't have a clue of that timeline then.

Two months in, I had to confess to myself that I was a comfort-driven woman. I have to admit that when I made my first set of values, I actually wrote comfort as one of them. Then I looked at that and was like, "Oooh, that's not very edgy, in fact, that is kinda lame," so I changed it to something else. And yet I realized at that time that I truly was motivated by comfort in my life. Like with many realizations, a host of questions and emotions arose:

"How did I get to be this way? I'm pretty stumped and actually disappointed in myself. Is this a middle-aged thing? Am I lazy? Am I not really edgy at all but security and safety driven? Am I a big fake who seems rebellious yet doesn't like to get too cold and wet when I'm out hiking anymore? Am I more interested in feeding myself goodies and sleeping lots than being fueled by my passion and my gifts? I'm not liking how this notice is feeling...my choices are so influenced by physical, emotional, and spiritual comfort. Egads, who have I become? And the bigger question: what am I going to do with this notice?"

All this questioning would soon be par for the course. And I began to learn how such questioning would lead to greater awareness and more questions.

Soon thereafter, my patterns around safety began to emerge. This would be the start of an ongoing exploration through the evolutions:

"I've been in a tender place this week with myself after exposing a life-long pattern of not feeling safe in the world. Seeing this is one thing...the healing will come as I begin to take the reins of my own sense of safety back. I realize that I hang onto every shred of safety I can find in the world while projecting and creating an alter-persona of brave, happy-go-lucky, wild woman-adventurer. And I am that, too. And I am also a tiny scared little girl who wants to feel safe."

Ah, the beginning of the personal hell spiral of the first evolution. I began to cultivate a perspective where I could observe myself and my behaviors with interest but without investment. In other words, my awareness was such that I would see my stuff, even while not being in a place to transform it yet. That can be an unpleasant, devilish place, a good time to want to run away, which is one of my primary strategies that I employ to avoid just about everything unpleasant.

But there is no avoiding your stuff if you are on the path to transformation.

4 months in and I started spiraling through some major fear. "I am pretty much losing my shit right now. It's not pretty in my life right now. Patterns are flowing thick and I'm not doing too well with accepting the changes. Damn. I knew it'd get tough but...ugh." After this dramatic statement, I felt a little embarrassed but also proud that I didn't keep my experience to myself, as was my normal pattern of silent suffering. I knew that momentum and transformation didn't always look or feel nice and comfy. I was allowing the discomfort and terror of change to coexist with the glory of a bigger, better, more me.

Then, towards the end of the first evolution, I had this amazing experience. A simple thing, really, but it struck me how grounded I had been feeling by that time

"This past weekend, a woman was sitting across the table from me demonstrating a concept with some pill bottles. She accidentally knocked them all across the table and into my lap. I didn't flinch or move at all. This felt like a personal triumph. When my anxiety was higher and my nervous system amped up, I would have jumped at things flying into my lap, even innocuous pill bottles. I would have been more reactionary and on edge. I felt that not overreacting to something that wouldn't hurt me means I'm moving in the right direction where my nervous system reacts in accordance with the level of threat."

Badassery starts in small moments of personal triumph, like not overreacting to flying salt shakers.

Evolution Two
Donnaah

Evolution 2 was focused on breaking patterns and developing deeper self-awareness. It is one thing to see your patterns and be repulsed or terrified or confused or determined to break them. It is a whole other thing to actually go about the work to break the patterns that are so engrained in your being, your body, your emotions, your subconscious, your nervous system.

I began to devote to doing the micropractices on a daily basis in a new way. For the first time in my life, I was doing things supportive of me every single day that wasn't about constant exercising, working, inhabiting my marriage, or being a foodie. I began to show up for myself in ways that only I could feel, and I was being accountable to me and my tribe. This had a huge impact by the end of this evolution.

First, a short story of overcoming sudden illness that occurred soon after this evolution began:

"I was out backpacking with my hubby at a glorious and very remote spot. We were 9 miles from the trailhead with melting snow and mixed terrain. As I started to hike out, I suddenly felt very ill. And immediately my mind wanted to start spinning worse case scenarios. I sat down and breathed for a while, acknowledging the illness but not allowing panic to worsen my condition. Then I expressed gratitude for my strong legs, knowing they could carry me out safely.

I listened to what my body needed which was movement. Even when my hubby took a break to eat, I kept moving, slowly and steadily through the cycles of nausea. I looked up at the treetops and gazed at the beauty all around me. I breathed with my steps like a lengthy walking meditation. And I made it out and eventually felt much better by the last night.

I was proud of my self-care and, as I said to my hubby, "If I'd allowed my head to take over, I'd still be sitting on the trail crying and paralyzed with fear." Instead, I circumvented that whole deal by breathing, insourcing what my body needed from moment to moment, and staying present to the reality of my situation, which was: I felt horrible, but I could breathe and walk."

So, this was such a beautiful experience for me, despite the pain. I could feel my body giving me information and ultimately felt this was a practice opportunity created by my body in cahoots with the universe. I felt powerful to not launch myself into a scary, pity party but to be curious and non-judgmental about how I was feeling and to rely on my body's ability to give me information to support whatever was happening at the time. Strangely, it ended up being a really wonderful experience. It was lovely, in a way, to allow rather than resist the illness. Talk about present moment!

Then, less than a month in to the second evolution, this happened: "My husband has asked me for a divorce today. I am challenged to accept this."

I was shocked. But with the new patterns of self-care, action, resilience, and awareness, by the next day, I was feeling stronger and committed to breaking the damn victim pattern I seemed to always fall into. I was safe and knew I'd be okay." This new development gave me the perfect storm in which to practice my evolving ways of doing and being in the world. All of me was suddenly called into full-on play.

With this immense shift in my reality, I launched into action. Within weeks, I moved out of my beautiful home, started couch surfing between friends' houses with me my 2 beloved Weimaraners, moved my things into storage, gotten an attorney, and presented my husband with a petition for divorce.

In the face of courageous and focused action, my practices, which I had so devotedly adhered to previously, became sporadic. I fell behind on practically everything in my life except self-care, which I cranked even higher. I felt grounded and fierce and peaceful and focused.

"I am going to own this divorce. I am taking the reins. I have amazing support and community. My intention is to receive from others and to be witnessed through this process. I am feeling such abundance, love, tenderness, care. I am beyond thankful that I am working every day to move the energy, to create momentum, to blaze my path, to open to possibility."

During this time of dissolution, one month into this evolution, and I began to notice a unique aspect of my own brand of life mastery that started to appear as a result of the massive changes and letting go I was doing in the wake of the separation and leaving behind security and comfort. My super special energetic talent for emptiness began to emerge:

"I've spent most of my life fleeing empty and yet also being afraid of full. So, I have been lingering in middle land of not too empty and not too full. I used to pack my life absolutely full out of fear of emptiness, which I believed meant starvation, lack, void.

I'm finding now that empty is suiting me in this time of transition. The more empty the house is, the better I feel. I've been eating little and actually feel more healthy and energetic. My mind has moments of sweet emptiness. And I am finding a clarity that has escaped me in the past. From the emptiness, the unknown feels less scary, like I can slip easily through the challenges and not get stuck in the fullness of the details."

Then another pattern came up that I began to break: "Just play it nice and get it over with." This usually would show up during tense, unpleasant conversations with family members, in particular. What I began to notice was my ability to speak my truth and set clear boundaries even in the midst of noticing I wanted to check out and just get through the conversation. And with just a couple of breaths after such events, I was able to dispel the tension and move on with my day. I was able to do this because my body was beginning to relax and my anxiety, lower, such that, when stressors did occur, they didn't sink in and cause me to start looping like before. I was able to face my stressors with well-honed tools, a modicum of grace, with a dollop of courage.

My motto those days (and still my motto now) is: Bring It On. There is so much more.

About 3 months into evolution 2, I began to spontaneously practice manifesting abundance through trust and intention. There was all manner of crazy abundance showing up in my life as I shifted away from being stuck and as I let go of what I thought was security and safety. My house sold in less than 2 weeks for significantly more than the realtor suggested because I intuited a sale price and my soon to be ex-husband agreed to list at that price. I had a job offer land in my lap out of the blue for contract work at a significantly higher wage than I was currently working at. And one day after I set the intention for a house to rent, a coworker called me to tell me that he has a place opening next month that is perfect and is willing to rent it to me month to month, dogs welcome, and an affordable rent.

Wow. Magical became my go-to word.

And then as the legal process of divorce started to feel real to me, I began to deeply grieve the ending of my 10-year marriage. I was amazed that I could be angry yet not reactionary, to be conscious and clear, even in the midst of intense grief and sadness. I kept looking for the lessons and why these twists and turns were showing up for me, why I had chosen to engage in this energy. It was pretty cool to be curious while pissed off, to be looking for deeper meanings when I wanted to hit things. Through all of this crazy ass journey, I kept reminding myself that I can be all things and that I love myself.

3 months after the separation began, courageous action and insourcing was par for the course now as I prepared to move to a city that I knew nothing about, into a house with just me and my dogs. I was finding myself inordinately excited by this immense opportunity for self-reliance and self-sufficiency. Even though I had I lived by myself for many years before my marriage, this felt different, like a chosen adventure, a calling to be free of all that was, a calling towards the unknown and undiscovered within:

"I am feeling how I want to choose what components of my life I want to carry forward and what I want to let go...noticing how many relationships I want to let go and how curious and eager I am to find new tribe. I am enticed by how loneliness will fill me up. I am intrigued by the idea of creating my own set of daily rituals and practices. I am ready to dive into a new level of soul work and hone my skills around the creation of me. It's terrifying and exhilarating at the same time. All I can say is that there is no question this is my next step."

How did I know without question about my next step? It was totally insourced.

4 months into Evolution 2, I began to think about hope, the energy of hope. And I realized that I just didn't like it. In my book, it was like trying: it wasn't a real thing. It's a distraction so I could feel like I was doing something. When I lived in hope, I felt that I was moving away from what was real for me in the present moment by shifting my energy to a place that didn't exist and might never exist except in my mind. I understood that only when I took action did I manifest what I wanted in my life.

Hoping for something to magically happen or appear was poor energy management and disconnected me from loving my present life. So, I set an intention to invest all that wandering, hoping energy into realness and into intentionally taking action to create the life I desired.,

One year into this work, early in 2015, I began to lose track of time as I moved out of a brain- and thought-focused existence. Words seemed to escape me at times. I wrote:

"I am living life. Glorious, sacred, and profane...healing, playing, and letting go, letting go, letting go...Lessons are thick these days. Falling apart and feeling serene at the same time. In sourcing is my savior, despite my near total lack of micropractices, although I have to say that drinking a beer while meditating on Mama Gaia or basking in the sun admiring my soft belly or watching the lily pads open while listening to the crash of waves are all micropractices in my book.

I am listening carefully to the whispers and shouts of my Soul and I'm devoted to following her path of uncertainty and bliss and wildness and gifts… I am feeling the pull of my truth, am setting delicious boundaries, and creating space for whatever comes through… So many flexible pieces in my life to play with and rearrange…Sacred Nos and Sacred Yeses fill me up."

I was learning my own way of insourcing, letting go of strictly following practices, and finding what worked for me.

Then, soon after this flying high phase, I woke up one day with what felt like a transformation hangover. It's like I woke up that day and truly felt all the changes I'd made in the past 6 months, physical, mental, spiritual, and emotional. I used breathwork to calm down. As old patterns dispersed, new patterns arose. Some of these new patterns were efficient use of my energy and masterful use of the micropractices to maintain my sanity and to manage the vast changes and energy flowing through me. Other patterns were more akin to evolved versions of previously challenging patterns. In this case, I first encountered a pattern I still carried with me, where I would expand and move into greater integrity through bold action and radical courage, only to find myself hungover in the wake of the transformation. It took a little getting used to, surfing my own unique waves of expansion and finding a new normal but with awareness comes mastery.

A little over a year in and I finally started to understand what Tanja had said probably a hundred times to me and my tribe. There isn't all this external energy that we must flow through us or bring to us or reach out for. The energy is all inside us. We are WAY bigger and expansive than we have known. It's all inside us. We are all of it already. I was beginning to finally feel that at moment what insourcing was really about – not just awareness of the energy within me but knowing that there was nothing from the outside needed to tap into that inner energy.

As things progressed with the divorce, the emotional turmoil took its toll. I didn't like how it was going. Of course, what is there to like about divorce? It was a most frustrating mess of a process and I found myself holding my Self literally and figuratively amidst triggers and reactions and emotions that came up unbidden when I had to communicate with my someday-will-finally-be-my-ex. I would be floating along happily in my new, lovingly designed life and then he steps in and boom! the perfect trigger into old patterns of victimhood and icky strategies in the face of his demands, impatience, and total inability to consider my view or even my existence.

That was a hard time. I wanted to sound all evolved and benevolent but there was vast fury and grief that cycled through me. It fed my growth as I felt it, allowed it, and waved it goodbye until the next meeting. It took me out at the knees at times. But I had so many tools that I felt ready for the next travesty, the next blow, the next gruff word. I was so thankful for micropractices, macropractices, energetic awareness, and massive self-care and self-love to get me through each day, each night, each storm that soon passed. I was learning to ride the waves.

My new mantra became: I know what I want. That is all I need to do, keep knowing what I want.

One practice of this work involves decluttering, letting go of those things that do not serve you, which anchor you to staying stuck, which take up space in your life to the detriment of the new coming in. At this point, I had let go of my house and much stuff. I had let go of friends and family members and physical preoccupations. Now, a new layer presented itself:

"I had a total meltdown, the good kind, last night over finally saying good-bye to Seattle. I realize that I can have projections even onto a city, a land, a place. And today somehow this has morphed into unfollowing tons of "friends" on FB. I've been unsubscribing like crazy from newsletters and groups as well. Ahhh, decluttering, layer upon layer...The more space, I create, the better I feel. And the more space I have to do whatever the hell I want, to design a life full of whatever feels good to me, because that is all I have to do right now."

I began to experience a sense that who I am evolves day to day. I had let go and was letting go of so much and had no idea where was going. There wasn't a plan. I totally trusted in mystery to guide me and was opening to the greater vision of my soul rather than coming from my too-tiny, way-limited intellect. There was so very much and so very little that I wanted. I wanted clarity and energy mastery above all else, and I wanted to be reorganized at a cellular level for optimal thriving and full creative expression of my unique self and soul in this life. And I wanted a quiet life right of integrity and energetic alignment. And more than anything at that moment, I wanted to be outside and watch the sunrise and sunset. That made each day complete for me

A new level of insourcing began to take hold in me, where something I knew in my head as a truth became integrated into my body as truth. Then, when that happened, there was no longer any question of the knowing, the truth.

And my relationship to comfort was continuing to shift, ever since I had declared it as one of my values. Now I started feeling into the balance between comfort that serves me and comfort that limits me. For example, asking myself, "What the meaning is for all my stuff. Did I love all of my stuff or was I just comfortable with it?" I realized that there is a shadow aspect to every value that I declared. For example, the comfort of my physical body helped me to go deeper into my edge and to allow discomfort in other areas of my life. Yet, I found that I had a belief that I needed to be tougher than that and thus I would tend to discount how physical comfort actually supports me. I realized that I did not need to suffer in order to expand and grow.

And this fed into my growing understanding of personal safety. For me, I was able to tolerate the tension and discomfort that accompanies growth. I could allow that when I felt that my body was safe. And of course, I created my own sense of safety. I wrote this to my tribe:

"I know when I have created safety for myself when I feel safe: my body is relaxed, my anxiety is low, and I trust in my knowing that all is well. A good practice that got me started with feeling my own created sense of safety is asking myself "Am I safe in this moment?" especially in moments when I am triggered. Thing is, feeling unsafe is also a created experience, generally from my thoughts and beliefs. "Oh, that {fill in the blank} looks scary so I don't feel safe." versus "Oh, that {fill in the blank} looks scary and it doesn't affect my personal sense of safety because I know I am flexible, adaptable, not at true physical risk, and I trust my awareness and intuition to guide my actions in this moment."

So, I was gaining and practicing an insourced sense of safety rather than relying on others or external circumstances to provide me with a sense of safety. From that place of self-trust, I could tolerate and allow discomfort and edgy growth.

Evolution Three
Donnaah

Evolution 3, which began about 14 months after the start of Evolution 1, was focused on relating to others and speaking our truths. I started out with an evaluation of my values list, the one from List 1, and I wrote about how each was showing up for me in my life at that point:

Freedom: My whole life is cultivating freedom in terms of spaciousness right now. I don't do social events. I've let go of most of my friends. I don't really go anywhere except where I want to go. I don't do but what I'm drawn to do. I'm practicing being unreliable. I live in a town where no one knows me, so I am free to be whoever I want, which is no one. I listen to my soul and follow the thread. I've been playing with emptiness, which to me is a type of freedom. I'm on the verge of letting go of all romantic (emotional) attachments. I have this sense that there is something coming for/to/towards me so I am creating space for it, whatever it is, to be free to open fully to it. Ultimately, I am free to be me, do me, follow only me.

Authenticity: This one has been showing up bigtime recently, particularly in the emergence of a remembered/allowed forthright, almost brash side of me. I am not so nice, in fact,

I'm actively allowing the not-so-nice parts of me to show up and be spoken. This is an important part of authenticity for me: to be all of me, to allow all of me to roam and muck things up, especially the parts I've been hiding/suppressing. I ain't so pretty right now and I'm good with that...kinda bull-in-the-china-shop at times....

Awe: Every day, I get up early and watch the sunrise. Awe in a nutshell, daily. There are add-ons every day but this sets the stage for each day.

Adventure: I've painfully admitted to myself recently that I have let the athletic adventurer part of me go by the wayside. I hardly hike anymore. I don't have any desire, strange to say, to travel. I'm discovering a vast adventure of places never trodden before within me. It's way edgy. To me, adventure is guided by curiosity and I'm way curious about myself and my inner journey and all the nooks and crannies I find along the way.

Beauty: I watch my dogs snore = beauty. I gaze at the peas sprouting in my backyard = beauty. I spend time every day sitting and watching and feeling the energy of beauty and divinity around me. I see beauty. I feel beauty. I am beauty-full.

Self-love/compassion: I'm humbled by the depths of love I am finding for myself as I get quieter, stiller, more watchful, and more aware. As the deeper shadow parts come up to play, I find self-compassion is absolutely necessary...else, I'd probably be totally depressed and shocked by the "not-me."

My new mantra became: I don't have to DO anything to belong. Belonging is how I feel inside.

After the divorce mediation, it became: The story of me in my own heart is the only one that matters.

And, as usual for me, as I expanded, I encountered my transformation hangovers. There were times when I felt like I was teetering on an edge, not quite able to calibrate myself between worlds. And then I would look in the mirror and recognize myself for the first time in what felt like ages. I'd feel like a hot mess. And my reaction during this time was "UGH...like, really? This is what it takes?! Whew, man, surrender ain't all pretty and wahoo. It's a bit nauseating." And of course, my next reaction would, "Bring it on, hell, what do I have to lose but everything?"

A month later, mid 2015, and I wrote this:

"I feel more like me than ever before. I feel that being ever more integrated and living within my values, speaking my truth, having confidence, and allowing myself to be guided by my Soul on my own unique journey means that I am in alignment and that brings clarity which opens the opportunity for God/Mystery/Universe to easefully bring goodness into my life.

I feel free, so unattached to plans or outcomes or the choices of others. Yet my whole life now is shifting and rotating slowly towards one of service to others. I don't even know what that means or looks like but it's exciting to me to be willing to be repulsed and rejected along the way. I am loved. I matter. It is pretty awesome."

And still, I kept taking radical courageous action. I turned in my resignation for one of my contract positions yesterday. I'd been out of integrity for a while there and I'd known it but I had kept hiding out and "getting by." I openly admitted that I was lost and didn't want to catch up with the technology there. I felt immense gratitude for the kindness and understanding they showed me through my divorce. And I was ready to part ways. So, with trepidation and knowing, I went back to part-time work.

In the midst of all this expansion and congruence, a new vision came through for me. This was going to call forth huge courageous action from me. I started to get rid of much of my stuff and put the rest in storage as I felt a calling to take off in the Fall for a cross country wander, eventually ending up in NC for the winter. I was planning to return to the state where I grew up, after 20 years, a trial run at entering back into the family dynamic. I had no idea how long I would stay there. My life was totally open-ended at that point and this calling had come to me, amongst many other revelations, during my Vision Quest.

And this vision absolutely terrified me. I could feel how much easier it would be to stay in my awesome little house in Tacoma and keep on learning and isolating and enjoying the sweet life I'd created there. But I could not do that. Holy crap, the pull was strong to stay but I knew I had to leave. I could feel the energy swirling in me around this move, intoxicating and powerful. That also scared me a bit.

I felt like I had no idea what I was doing. I didn't. I was following my heart and Soul. And they don't think.

But with the tools and practices that I had cultivated, I was grounded and prepared, even as I went through cycles in my relationship with my personal unknown, from full embrace/WAHOO to ugh/really?! I did not know what/where/how I would be and that was cool with me. I knew only what I was called to in this moment, which was to go back to NC for a while after a wander across the country.

I was beginning to notice how the separation between my body and my mind was becoming less pronounced. I had this shock when I thought about how in the past I have tended to inhabit my body with my mind rather than truly living in my body. Like my body isn't just a container for my mind and all these separate aspects of me but I am my body as much as I am my mind and soul. I was feeling into a deeper place around this, like the integration of body and mind was starting to be less a concept and more of a way of life. Like the edges were blurring.

And with this came another realization: that feeling special and different had kept me separate from myself, from my emotions, from others, and from the depths. Like, no one could ever understand me or love me or truly see me because I am so unusual, weird, whatever, so I'll just hang out over here by myself, so I don't have to risk being rejected or disappointed. While all the time, inside, the screaming says, "Love me." I no longer wanted to be special. I wanted to be love. Thing is, we are ALL special and different. We know this (yeah yeah) but to truly feel it as truth and act from that place is something else.

Being special isn't an unusual type of wounding. It is the essence of humanity, of being alive.

By July 2015, I had a new understanding of how I operate best in the world and in my life: I am never so happy as when in motion. The tension created by motion, by being betwixt and between, is what kept me going, on one hand. I also knew how non-motion was deeply restorative, on the other hand. I tended then and now to live in the paradoxes and I like it there. I found joy in solitude without lovers and in connection with many lovers. I found joy sitting on my backporch listening to the birds and in the middle of a raucous crowd. I was ever changeable, and this was my joy. The more I embraced my changeable nature, my flexibility and adaptability, the more I loved myself and the more I could love others.

Even with my successes, awareness of pesky persistent patterns often came through. I noticed, for examples, that I was still craving external validation, even as I was getting comfortable with aloneness and loneliness. I was still seeking validation in some ways from the few people left in my life and it felt icky because it revealed my patterns of outsourcing and playing nice. I really wasn't that nice, but I still presented that way for those I love. I was getting very tired of that. Like, sooooo tired.

As often was the case, it was a matter of taking bold action and I could feel the words I needed to say to those people. I was even dreaming the words. I often felt like I was practicing in my sleep sometimes. I was very tired of the turmoil I created inside by resisting the action, by not being current, by ignoring what I knew I needed to do because a pattern was running me.

At some point, the resistance wasn't worth it anymore. The payoff wasn't even fun anymore. Whatever the payoff was paled in the face of being authentically and wholly me.

This evolution was about speaking our truths. And the more I spoke my mind, my truth, without the filter of the Good Girl, the more I liked myself. It felt good to speak the truth of what was current. It was different than my ideas or perhaps ideals of myself, but it is where I was. I actually felt relieved to say, "I'm not that anymore and it's okay." When I wasn't speaking my truth, I was sacrificing my needs. And that gave off the decaying smell of martyrdom and energy of emotional turmoil. And my values definitely did not include turmoil.

My ultimate question was really, "How far out of integrity was I willing to go to get my needs met?" Because it is a choice I was making each time I didn't speak my truth or ask for what I desired. Each time I noticed a lack of truth speaking, it was time for action. My life was all about movement now. Stagnation or putting anything important to me on the backburner was not in integrity for me.

There was a growing fierceness and fearlessness within me. I felt a little reckless at times, not that my behavior showed it so much. It was more of an inner state. It was like a combination of freedom and surrender/abandon tempered by a moral compass and self-trust with an edge of Whattheheck. I felt a little crazed at times although my energy was mostly calm. Paradoxical as usual.

It was so freeing to not claim to be consistent or to make sense. I was sure that I sounded confused and off kilter at times because I was. It was the kind of murkiness that comes when I quit trying to control, impress, or resist and to move beyond illusion and pattern. I just didn't know what was there because it was new territory for me. I was giving myself total permission to not keep it together and thus was sorta all over the place. I welcomed flying by the seat of my pants at this time.

Then, along came another thought: I had been so involved in dismantling and letting go and creating space that I hadn't been visioning what I was growing into. There was the other side of letting go and that was what I thought I was moving towards, what I was consciously creating.

My challenges included staying in my body, grounding. At least I was no longer flying off away from my body as I had earlier that year (and for most of my life). I was feeling a deeper grounding, even as I had intense times of panic and fear and generally feeling like I was a pain in the ass to everyone who loved me...even as I felt a new way of being me, of walking as me, unapologetic and knowing and yet totally in the practice field of newness. It was an amazingly tender and powerful time for me.

And I began to realize that the setting the intention and setting boundaries were incredibly important components, to move from an understanding of my values and needs into action. However, the boundaries I set could be as permeable and flexible as love and kindness and intuition needed them to be.

In other words, I could live from intention, but I didn't have to be a hardass about them. Holding on with rebellious energy to what I have decided I needed to do was a big pattern that needed to die, too.

Again, there were the days when I woke up very tired, a bit scared, and empty. Breaking any pattern leaves a gap in how I had been walking in the world, a break in the known and familiar of me. I could always feel how easy it would be to pick it back up and at the same time I could feel this was no longer an allurement, not an option.

There really is no going back when we commit to freeing ourselves and living in integrity. There is only now and the next now. Letting go of the stories of who we were may take a little time and I would feel the grief of ending a sweet dream.

But then, I would think, "Fuck that! What was sweet about that dream? What of those stories are worth repeating? I walked away from connections and things that no longer serve me and I rock. We are all catalysts for ourselves and others in this life. Even saying all this is a pattern. I do not need to wallow and worry. I embrace the unknown with all of my heart. Heck yeah."

I had started noticing how I had lived in a protective stance, in fear, a layer of tension right under my skin, like survival energy, fight or flight, ready position anticipating attack. I felt this layer dissipating. It was truly amazing to feel how I'd carried this legacy of fear and protection and how I was letting it go now. My body felt dissonant and calm and stirred up and grounded.

And another layer of protectedness was showing itself, too. I noticed that even my thoughts could be protective. As in, anticipating a reaction, situation -- I noticed that even anticipating or expecting or predicting a possible scenario could be stressful to my body and being.

For example, just anticipating that my family would not accept me, even putting that scenario out on the table, so to speak, was stressful. This was not being current. In the current moment, my family was not rejecting me. It was possible that they would and yet any energy I put towards that possibility was truly wasted and in fact stressful because my thoughts would be manipulated by the prediction of future fear. So, as I was releasing the energy of holding myself ready for attack, I also was noticing I need to not be attacking myself through these types of thoughts. Dang hard pattern to break, that one.

As 2015 started to wind down, I was thick in the process of packing and moving and so many changes. I was living in a great harmonious mix of self-care and asking for help and decluttering and saying no and finding joy in small moments and mourning. I described my general state of existence this way:

"It's chaos, but good chaos, like whirling in a circle while dancing. The more I get out of my way and surrender to the process, the better I feel. I've let go of the illusions about what this trip home will be. Each time I think of how it may be, I feel how that imbalances me. I am open to what will be when it is, rather than spinning my energy and thoughts out ahead of me.

What's amazing is that I have this growing sense of my power, as in, I am a powerful human being, a powerful healer, a powerful light in this world. I don't really have to do anything but be me to be powerful. I feel energy in subtle ways around me, requiring fewer cosmic 2x4s to get my attention. Or maybe it's just that the cosmic 2x4s aren't such a big deal anymore. Like, oh yeah, I see you...cool."

I gave away most of my things and stuff and furniture. I packed what was left in storage. I hitched up my trailer and my 2 dogs and hit the road. I was so very tired. And it wasn't just the rigors of the road. I woke up one morning with the thought that I was not being responsible for my gifts, for my medicine, for who I was becoming. I was not giving myself the space and time and quiet for emergence.

Why do I always seem to choose trial by fire? It seems my soul was calling me to that. I was feeling more and more how my path ahead is not oft-traveled. I felt how I was still holding onto my small life. I wanted to say that I was falling apart. Perhaps that is what needed to happen. Perhaps I needed to let go of even more of who I thought I was. There was more to radical freedom than I could ever imagine.

By November 2015, I dragged out my original list of needs to reexamine. I'd been pretty solid on my original list of values for some time, but I made a few changes. Values: Freedom, Authenticity, Intuition (was Awe), Curiosity (was Adventure), Self-Love/Compassion, Courage (believe it or not, this wasn't on the original list...was Beauty). The addition of courage was huge for me. Like, duh. But still, huge.

My original list of needs from evolution one was huge. Looking at them all now, I thought, "This is a load of crap." They sounded good (what exactly does a need for "serving the highest good of myself and others" mean?!) but by this time I'd realized that my needs were actually pretty basic: time in Nature, lots of self-care, connection to soul, to feel loved, and continuous growth and expansion.

Coming into integrity with my true needs felt so much better. And with the letting go of lofty needs came this rumination over lofty intentions:

"I was thinking this morning on my walk that lofty intentions sure keep me stuck, thinking I am not enough, not doing enough, not being enough, always out of reach. Loftiness by definition means out of reach for me. Yet we are constantly fed these ideas that we are supposed to do all this and be all this for others when most of us can't even be and do for ourselves. So we are totally ripping ourselves off by focusing on lofty intention, dream, visions, etc, when in fact we must start by getting down to earth, down and dirty, with ourselves first before we can ever begin to consider our purpose and place in the world. Lofty just seems like way too much energy."

After being back in my home state and with my family for a few weeks, I started feeling a lot around growing up and being an adult. I was feeling so over myself and wondering:

"Is this what it means to be truly an adult? To not need to feel special or to be noticed? And to choose to not engage in the drama? And to see how all the stuff I've been carrying around are really huge projections on my part onto those who are just living their lives and happen to be my blood relatives?"

Yes, I knew that there are patterns I was carrying from my childhood. But what I was seeing now was how I had chosen to take stories from my childhood and hardened them into facts about my adulthood. And as I looked at the basis of all the burdens I'd been carrying as truth in my life from my childhood, I was seeing how truly most of this was about me and my need to rebel and how this had sapped my vitality and isolated me from people who loved me. That said, I found myself seeing them clearly perhaps for the first time in my life and consciously saying, "I do not want that going forward."

So, the rebellion energy was morphing into clarity and consciousness and yet somehow, I felt rather blah about all of this. It didn't exactly feel like WOOHOO, which was strange. Usually I'd get all excited about AHAs and insight, but all of this felt deeper than that somehow. Almost like a big "ooooof". It was a big hit to my nervous system to see how I'd created this version of the dynamic in my head and had carried it around with me for so long.

My last day of age 48. I woke and cried for the loss of so much, feeling so much grief. Feeling how I was not sure how I am going to fill in all this space and emptiness with.

"Missing my old life. Knowing it's a pattern to look backwards with yearning. Feeling how kickassery isn't all wahoo. Feeling how I am growing up finally and how that isn't all wahoo either. Such a deep place of grief in my heart today. It's good. I am grateful to get real about how much I have let go and how much I have yet to create and knowing I have so much more to discover about what I want to create. I plan to do a lot of self-care today in this tender place. Inviting the tears because they reveal so much to me when I let them flow."

I started feeling how I needed to fully cultivate home within my body, to feel securely that I was home no matter where I roamed. And also, to be wherever I am fully. To listen to what the earth has to say to me wherever I go. I did enjoy, though, the sense of displacement, in a way. To not be so anchored to time and space. To feel how we create our environment and it is all just agreements and energy. The paradoxes in my life were thick and welcomed because they illuminated how much I am creator and manifestor of my life, if I just chose that.

And I began to laugh a great deal in those days, often in "inappropriate" situations. That was my Coyote nature coming through. And oh yes, the cosmic joke. She rocks. I feel like laughing is definitely a stress reducer too, letting off steam when I am under stress or feeling tense. I tended to laugh then (and still) when I see the ridiculousness of what is happening around me. Actually, I'd always been like that, laughed like that. But now I began to not suppress it so much.

As I had arrived back to the family fold, I realized that being rejected by my family was the most primal survival fear I could think of. This was based on a value I was given as a child -- family/blood is the most important thing. But Family had never been my own value (or so I thought). Getting real with all this stuff that wasn't mine and never was mine was a little terrifying and yet I felt exhilarated too. Who was I without all these strings attached to me?

As evolution 3 came to a close, I was feeling like I was really falling apart or was it cracking open or was it letting go? I felt this thing like an earthquake inside. Panic and terror and curiosity and knowing, all mixed up and showing me AHAs. Like, I couldn't do small talk anymore. It felt like a lonely place in the world when I couldn't express myself. And I would feel such pain. It was psychic or spiritual, but I could feel it in my body almost as physical pain. It was pretty strange to feel it so excruciatingly, energetically. It was like my nervous system didn't know how to sort out different types of pain those days. It was a painful time in so many ways and yet such an expansive time for me. Hand in hand: pain and joy, contraction and expansion. I was truly beginning to understand that we are all things, we can be all things, everything all the time, all at once. It was exhilarating and terrifying.

Evolution Four
Donnaah

Two years into this work, Evolution 4 began. It was all about finding our passion and purpose in life. At that point, like for the previous levels, I was already deep into both of these journeys. Passion and Purpose were driving my explorations and my awarenesses.

And still, I continued to take small steps and bold actions towards clarity, understanding, and integrity with my truth, with my energy, becoming more and more the energy master that I so desired to be. As I reminded myself and others during this time: "Your mind doesn't want to change so even small things can feel like radical actions."

For example, I was supposed to go on a work trip at the beginning of this evolution and I really didn't want to go. It would've only been from a place of duty and "should." After a few other dramatic changes in plans resolved in my favor, I decided that the Universe really does want me to get what I want, if only I quit resisting how things looked like and how they would turn out and if only I would surrender to how things actually end up. In other words, instead of spending so much energy on pushing against what I didn't want, I decided to just keep in mind and stay focused on what I did want. So, I cancelled the work trip, lock stock and barrel. I felt empowered: This was in alignment with where I was going, and I was willing to look like a slacker or a loser, as long as I knew I am putting my oxygen mask on first.

This was one example of my experiments with the energy I call, "Death to duty!" As I began to learn how to no longer make plans from a place of duty, to start saying no again from the get-go instead of having to cancel plans previously made, I began to track how all these seeming obstacles were falling away.

From the get-go in this evolution, I continued expanding rapidly, cycling through moments like this:

"I woke up feeling itchy and discontented. Not physically itchy but spiritually itchy. Feeling like the changes I have made are radical, yes, but there is so much more. I feel this edginess that seems to show up when I start to do more practices and more ceremony. It's like, when I start to show up more for myself, I get more discontent and I see all the illusions more clearly."

Another cycle through the grips of "good enough" pattern emerged for me. I wasn't sure of the origin of this pattern and the attached belief system. And more importantly, I didn't need to logically understand it or figure anything out about it. The key to building integrity in my energy system was to be aware of it and move it through my practices and actions. I was feeling how limiting "good enough" had been in my life...just enough, good enough, no need to push beyond, or work too hard. It was like a damper that I'd put on my life, my love, my passion, all of me. Like a throttle – just enough to get by, to be okay.

Again, in this evolution, it was exactly that: an evolution, a spiral, a revisiting of the energies and awarenesses that had developed and been primed and explored in previous evolutions. This time, deepening and informing and inching me towards what was next. I had released so much of my identity and personas and almost all aspects of my previous life. I had gotten insight into patterns and strategies. Now I found myself in this place of not knowing who I was anymore. It was related to being quite emptied out, the boundaries and edges of me, undefined. I didn't know what I loved anymore. I didn't know what I wanted. My passion felt pretty tapped out.

And I was sitting in this place of "I have no idea" about my future. I no longer loved what I used to love, and I no longer wanted what I used to want. What would fill in my desires was still a mystery in many ways. I would have glimpses but mostly I continued to be adept and unfazed with dancing in the thick of the not knowing, a master of sitting with the unknown.

Around this time, I began to tackle a huge pattern of creating plans in order to feel like I am doing something. I have always been so good at getting things done. I call that part of me the "taskmistress." Thing is, when I make a plan then that becomes a story that I would find myself living into. I suppose that is what plans had been for me, to feel like I had some kind of direction.

It was subtle. Like I was so tempted for a bit to set an intention for the year to start knocking things off my bucket list. That felt like movement toward purpose for me at that moment but then I realized that really it was just a way to keep myself distracted from the now, to keep my brain occupied with logistics in order to feel like I was making some kind of progress, like that meant something, somehow, to complete my bucket list items.

Again, I learned to sit with the emptiness of the now and take just one step at a time. To discern truly what my next step was versus planning out a whole year of fabulous activities to occupy my egoself. The taskmistress in me died hard. I was up against the pattern of her - the one that wanted to arrange and organize and plan and then live into the story of what I had planned versus living life following what was TRULY alluring me in the moment. I understood that to follow allurement, to follow the threads of me, meant no planning, not even fabulous things. It meant taking the next step and moving slowly, listening, waiting until the next step was revealed. It was a dive into uncertainty and mystery.

I knew my next step at that point, of course I did. But everything after that that I had been planning (oh I'll go to Seattle for the summer and then and then) was just a story I was creating to keep myself entertained and feeling like I was not totally lost. But I was lost. That was the whole point. And it was good to be lost because from that place, there was much to be found. And thus, I began to see parts of my purpose, which was to follow mystery in my life and not let my plans become more alive than me.

And from that place of lost-ness, I began to ask and explore, "What does true freedom feel like and look like to me?" It was a slow revealing and I often wanted to return to aspects of my previous life. But going back to what was in any way, shape, or form didn't seem to fit into my desires to keep looking at my edges and busting patterns and staying uncomfortable and facing empty in myself.

Again, as in each evolution, I pulled out my values and needs to evaluate where I was right now, staying current with myself and the decisions I was making. I made a couple of small changes to them both. My current values were: Freedom, Authenticity, Intuition, Mystery (was curiosity), Self-Love, and Courage. I felt like at that time I was also making decisions from a desire for belonging or something akin to that, maybe related to my need to feel loved.

So now, as I was faced with making some new decisions in my current journey, I felt like it was good to check in with my values and needs because I wanted to stay in alignment and integrity with them. I felt a little rub around my value of Authenticity. There was a moment where I had self-censored that came to mind, a very small thing, but indicative. So, I began watching my relationship with true authenticity...what did that even mean to me?

Energetic transformation continued for me in this evolution. Moments when I would feel that something was not right with me today, like something was lurking inside that needed to be expressed. I would have agitated and wake up feeling like I had lived way too small my whole life, seeing so many memories and patterns in my past. Feeling like I am on some edge and wanting to coax out whatever was there.

Feeling that itchy feeling that came around for me every now and again. As I began to learn to tolerate these uncomfortable times, I would eventually transform, often integrating in sleep, sometimes waking up in the middle of the night almost unable to walk. I would have the prized moment when I woke and felt like a new person somehow...subtly so. I felt shifted, like I had new software operating within.

Then, 2.5 years into this work, I accepted a wild 30-day challenge. Throughout the evolutions, I had undertaken many 30 days challenges, doing some practice or awareness or activity every day for 30 days. There is a sense of empowerment and a feeling of vast personal integrity that develops, an unshakeable confidence in yourself that you can do anything you set yourself and mind and energy to when you accomplish 30 days without fail of doing something that, in the beginning seemed daunting but, in the end,, became easeful, even preferred.

I committed to doing 30 days of not speaking, 30 days of vocal silence. 30 days of limiting even written communications, a deep dive into emptiness and silence and inner quiet. I had just a few days to prepare – to tell my family, friends, even my dogs, that I wouldn't be available to speak for 30 days.

It was fascinating to step back and watch my strategies, reactions, and patterns coming up around this challenge before I had even begun it. Not to mention, the patterns and reactions and strategies of those around me, when I told them about this challenge, those who were directly impacted by my no talking challenge. I learned a lot about who was truly supporting me by presenting them with the information that starting tomorrow, I wouldn't be speaking to them or anyone for 30 days. No matter what.

And I had the perfect moment to watch my parade of strategies in a brilliantly abbreviated and accelerated pace: First, I said, "No way, impossible, I can't do it. Eeek, run away." Then I went straight to, "I'm gonna die." Then, because I am so clever and tricky, I thought "How can I negotiate my way out of this?" Then, I began to think, "OK, I can do this, but I must organize everything and strategize how to make this easy." I wanted to be in control of the experience. Then, a last-ditch bit of desperation showed up, "How can I hide for 30 days?" And then, finally, the ultimate place to which I needed to arrive: Surrender. Then, my brain said, "Okay, we're on." And, as always, the laugh came when I realized that I could check 30-day silent retreat off my bucket list!

All the journey of my 30 days can't be included here but I want to write a little bit about what came up for me as I moved into this new 30 days challenge initially, particularly around my values. I was walking my dogs just a day or so into the challenge, careful to not speak to them, when I realized something: I speak mostly to get what I want or to make others feel more comfortable.

And that point morphed into a consideration of my values. It became apparent to me that one of my values must be putting other people's comfort above my own, particularly because when I was presented with this challenge, my first thought was how not to inconvenience those in my life that I perceived as not being able to handle my choice to participate in this challenge. I went through a big shuffle of my plans and expended a lot of energy to connect with family before starting the challenge and thus to not expose them to the discomfort (nor did I have to be exposed to THEIR discomfort) over my challenge, particularly the awkwardness of being with them and not talking to them. I put what I perceived they needed to be comfortable ahead of my own needs.

So, I decided to be real and to own this value, as much as I didn't much like it. So now my values included not only hide myself in order to keep others comfortable, but also a greater realization that hit me like a ton of bricks: I realized I really do value my family. That in fact, one of my values (and this was a shock and came to be hugely transformative) was Family. I always considered family in my choices. I just hadn't let myself see this until now. Family was who I fled from, but I had never truly left them behind, even after 20 years in Seattle, 3000 miles away from NC.

And on top of all this, 2 weeks into my 30-day vocal silence challenge, I took off to drive solo across the country, pulling my vintage trailer with my 2 dogs. Cross country road trip in silence. Yeah, that was daunting: there would be so much more to navigate on the road by myself without speaking and I was feeling scared of that. At the same time, I was confident I could do it, but it seemed like so much work. As always, the resistance and anticipation created fear, a feeling of constriction in my energy and body.

During this challenge, I began to see how unconscious I become so quickly in so many ways throughout the day and how easy it was to want to speak without thinking. So, putting thinking before speaking was a great lesson but very tiring. I was beginning to prefer silence even though it could be super frustrating at times to not be understood and to not want to bother trying to be understood. So much surrender was needed. But also, I began to feel a super presence of mind and more connected to Mystery.

More realizations flowed in as my embrace of silence deepened, even to the point where I didn't laugh or whistle or hum. I began to understand how I used language to defuse situations, to self-soothe, to explode my shit all over the place. Anything but contain, which was what I was doing then.

I realized how much of my communication is really about connecting with others. And yet as I settled deeper into quiet, I was having moments when I wondered about my thoughts. It was hard to tell if they were thoughts or if I had spoken them. My thoughts were all I had, and I knew I wasn't speaking them yet there was some fine line that I couldn't quite distinguish, the boundary where thoughts become words and I was getting stuck in that place because they weren't becoming words. They were staying thoughts, which were ephemeral and thus it all seemed less real, undefined. It wasn't just vocal silence: it was non-communication in just about all forms. And I wasn't shut down so much as wide open.

That energy led to reflect on friendliness, a strategy I had employed to feel alive and not alone. I could see how I had been too approachable and perhaps gullible in my friendliness in the past. I was contemplating, "Who am I if I'm not friendly. A bitch? A loner? Boring?" These thoughts hit a lot of triggers, thinking I was being rude. But then again, was rude the result of non-friendliness? Seems like I thought it was, with my Southern upbringing, where being rude was inexcusable. Could I be wide open and not friendly? Could I not communicate and still project friendliness?

It was a constant experiment as I drove across the country, navigating campgrounds, roads, parks, and all the people randomly encountered along the way. I began to be comfortable just not answering the questions of strangers. And what I noticed was often it didn't matter anyway because they had an agenda in mind as they were talking to me so didn't seem to notice my lack of answers. What I came to sense was that my presence, my energy, my smile spoke enough. And that quiet is not as quiet does.

As the challenge continued, I began to notice that I was more patient and just dang happy. I had little interest in the future or the past. I could feel emotions associated with the past but without talking they didn't hold a lot of energy for me, they just passed. And if I thought about the future, well, again without talking, those thoughts didn't stick around.

Stories only become solid when fed, when given energy. Without energy, the thoughts or stories of what was or what might be weren't very nourished.

Thus, I was so happy because I was in the present moment, hanging out, not really doing much - not trying to accomplish much, express much, or learn much. Just kinda cruising. In the present moment, my thoughts sorta ran like this: "Food yum, Walk good, Dog happy." At times, I felt a little dumbed down but that wasn't a bad feeling at all.

Things get simplified when there is no way to enforce my agenda. More and more my life became about letting go of an agenda and just going with the flow. I felt happy. With me. Maybe not with all the fallout from my previous choices but in the present moment I was pretty content. And I had found that I was happy pretty much anywhere, too. I didn't want a home or partnership because I was pretty happy with anywhere and anyone. It's an inside job, happiness. And the less I talked, the more inside it became.

I realized that life doesn't need a running commentary. And I didn't need to justify my preferences or choices - I just needed to make them and then keep on going and living. As the challenge neared completion, I found myself feeling less affected by other people's states these days. I felt compassion, but I didn't need to shift myself to accommodate or meet their emotional states.

Then, suddenly, the challenge was done. Speaking was awfully weird and wonderful. I had the softest voice. I didn't feel particularly badass at the end of 30 days of silence, actively engaged in real, messy, full life in vocal silence. I did feel like a changed person and maybe that is badass!

Wrapping up evolution 4, I began to discover what lifestyle I truly wanted, what elements of a life I was wanting. I was getting pretty clear on them but without actively taking steps in that direction. I wasn't sure how it would all happen, given the possibility of caring for my grandmother starting in the fall of that year. I was happy and feeling integrated and at home...that is starting to be true wherever I go, no matter my circumstances. It is more about discernment about what I truly wanted and needed, conscious life-design. Who I was and who I was becoming and who I wanted to be. And with that, the realization that I needed to expand/recalibrate my own lifestyle and not continue to adapt to the lifestyles of others. Not to live within the confines of their lives. I needed to quit trying to create the life I wanted within the confines of the life I had. This was the perfect energy to move into Evolution 5.

Evolution Five
Donnaah

2.5 years from the beginning of this journey, Evolution 5 was focused on living courageously. Well, at this point, honestly for me, it was sort of a moot point. I was so far down the living courageously path that the focus for me was more around continuing to listen, act in accordance with my values, which includes and even highlights and even necessitates courage.

This is what I know about courage. You don't just magically come upon it as you go about your usuality or have it descend in a cloud from the heavens to bless your furrowed brow. You practice that shit. You cringe, and you ache and you cry and you do it anyways. You devote and you screw up and you redevote. Practice doesn't make perfect. Practice makes real and raw. It ain't sexy to think you must practice how you want to be but it's the truth of how you become. I know about courage because I live courageously.

Ever since I was separated, throughout the letting go and the wandering, I had been accompanied by my two loyal Weimaraners. Sara, the oldest, became sick during Evolution 4 with maybe cancer, definitely Inflammatory Bowel Syndrome. Then I had a brief brush with cancering uncertainty.

Illness, suffering, and as always, the thread of death and dying became more and more a part of my meditations and contemplations. I found that I didn't believe that my genetics were my life and death sentence. If so, I was pretty sure that I'd have been tanked already with heart disease, mental illness, diabetes, alcoholism, maybe a few I forgot, "in the family." I believe my perception and awareness can rewrite and rewire the responses and expressions of genes. For example, I knew in my life that my perception of safety caused less stress in my body.

I had been most always safe in just about any environment yet most of my life I had not felt safe because I hadn't trained myself to understand and trust the safety I now felt.

I continued getting a lot of clarity around lifestyle and self-management in the wake of my dog Sara's illness and slow, very expensive recovery. I had learned so many lessons through heartbreak but I then suddenly I realized: I have been focusing on the wrong things in my life. I had a moment when I woke up in the middle of the night (I had and still have many of such moments) with the thought, "I've been living my life all wrong." Now, I meant wrong for me in that moment. Following Mystery takes a lot of faith and trust and the choices made from those energies were clear. But I was getting lots of information from my heart and soul that I wasn't acting on that then seemed to come around to bite me. I needed to slow way down (even more) and listen to the subtle energies way more.

And I saw that I needed to start living the life I wanted, doing the things I wanted to do, being how I wanted to be instead of waiting for a partner or life situation or financial goal or anything else external to me to show up and prompt me in those directions. I was so ready to be solo and settle and make a life for me. I could feel that I would still wander on the land, but a home base was calling me. I began to suspect that sometime in next year I would create a home for me. And I was right.

But as always, divine timing was taking the time I needed to continue to integrate and awaken to greater integrity and soul understanding before I found the place to settle.

I spent a fair bit of time in this evolution doing 30-day challenges and making dietary changes and micromanaging my energies. Then, I had an awakening around the 30-day challenge practice. I'd done many successful 30-day challenges. And whenever I again felt a real need for something that I believed would expand me then I will happily undertake one. But to continue doing them, just to do them, well, I realized that that didn't really serve me right then. I had been putting in place so many rules and practices that my inner taskmistress was very thrilled to have something to do all the time. And my straight A student was very happy to successfully complete all these practices and challenges.

However, I now felt like I was moving into a more integrated space, a place I had previously been, but then had started layering lots of to do's every day on top of and regressed back to a pattern of pleasing my inner taskmistress. So, I threw out all the rules and suggestions and practices and I started to let them flow through as needed. I began to trust in my intuitive knowing of the self-care I most needed and the practices that were most supportive. I no longer needed to schedule and monitor them so closely. They were actually such a part of me that managing them felt fake, unauthentic, and forced.

Where I was (and continue to be since then) was very much in flow and feeling rather free. At that time, I was curious to see how I would sustain myself without the must dos of practices every day. This was my journey, and this was what I was choosing. This was a deeper level of devotion to the inner listening to myself and to trust that this work lives with me and within me and that I embody it. I was finding that living in gratitude took me a long way each day towards bliss.

As with each evolution, I revisited my values and needs. This 5th evolution, I felt like I was getting much closer finally to my true set of values: Freedom, Authenticity, Courage, Self-Love/Compassion, Listening to Mystery, Intuition, Family (I was still letting that one sink in). My Needs were spot-on by now and led my daily life choices: Time in Nature every day, connection to Soul, to feel Loved, Continuous expansion, walking 5 miles a day, good sleep hygiene, and lots of self-care (spinal work in particular). And, one postscript to my needs: I really needed my bare feet on the ground every day.

I continued to wonder, what was the next level for me? What did I feel called towards in my life right now? What would the next level of life mastery feel like to me? My answer kept coming up like this:

"I am wanting to step into deeper service, collaboration, and co-creation with others in business and personal vision. I want to bring all of me to the table in all aspects of my life. It's not that I need to let go of anything more but rather to start building more depth into my personal connections, creating tribe and community."

This claiming, to be of service, was a new dawning for me. I had discovered that a lot of my recent life I had isolated. I had taken time to grieve and let go and get current and feel everything and create space and embraced emptiness. And yet what I was discovering was in fact that I was fueled by connection with others. Any other people, it didn't even have to be tribe or like-minded folks. Just others. I became aware that I was ripe and ready to come out of my shell and be seen in whole different way, to bring connection to a new level for myself via community and service and friendship and letting go of my agenda – that was what all of this had been about. For me, it had been easy to deepen into practices and let go of service to the world. Now I was ready to forge my own way in the world of people again.

And I began to see how I tended to manifest situations that gave me specific information to work with over and over in my life. It was fascinating to live in this place where I could watch myself in these situations. It was like the Universe said, "Here, chew on this." And then I got to unpack the episodes and look for patterns and triggers and make new choices. It was like exercising new muscles, integrity muscles. And this often came as a feeling of being out of integrity and that feeling would inform me as to where I was in relationship to life mastery at that time. In other words, when I could feel that I was out of integrity, this was actually a call towards greater life mastery. I thrived in that place, living on that edge, the discomfort but always the huge awareness to be gained from the discomfort. It was suggested to me that it was a place of purposeful struggle.

I did feel that, purposeful struggle happening for me -- watching old stories and strategies and patterns surface, getting my attention through emotion, and then moving aside as I faced them, unresisting. It's a fascinating experience (and also a bit tiring). There were moments when I felt I wanted to chuck it -- such an old pattern that working at something isn't worth it when I am constantly on my edge.

I had disavowed the word "struggle" in my vocabulary years ago and was wary of it when I heard others use it. Generally, we aren't struggling in the pure sense of the word. Our first world problems aren't struggles. I felt like using the word "struggle" created drama and a sense of hopelessness or perhaps a lack of devotion. So, I reframed this into a phrase that felt more congruent for me, "purposeful engagement." I had had a feeling of being out of integrity, but I realized that actually this was actually a call to a higher level of mastery. I had to watch my own cleverness, where I could use my self-knowledge and level of integration to keep myself stuck by saying, "Oh that isn't in my value system" or "I am out of integrity, "when in fact I was being stretched, expanded, and challenged by my own soul. Again, the gifts were so worth the discomfort when I sat with it.

I continued to explore what I was wanting -- I was wanting something more for me, something to feel passionate about and to occupy my energy. And where I was in my personal evolution, one thing I did know was that it wasn't going to a relationship that filled me up. It was gonna be passion, mission, purpose, spirit, mystery.

And yet still at that time, I felt stuck in how to create more of all of that in my life. Partly it was my wandering lifestyle -- wandering meant that I was always having to uproot, adapt, be flexible, move on. Partly it was old strategies that I was still moving through, more subtle layers of introspection and awareness. Partly, I was in a place of feeling kinda blah. This was familiar to me as the blahs tended to happen when there weren't drama, distractions, and stories to fill up my mental energy. And partly it was feeling less vital from all the physical disruption in my body.

But I understood that ultimately this was really all about me. I had been redefining who I was becoming and how I wanted to live my life. After a year and a half since my divorce, I was finally really looking at what was next for me, after this wandering stage, and things were starting to feel real around that. And I had energy to devote to what I wanted, whenever I did get very clear on what that was.

In the meanwhile, I was engaged with looking at my patterns of focusing on relationship over my mission and also my current priority of finding purpose. I wanted both relationship and purpose and was learning how to manage my energy and surrender to passion and to my mission while still staying engaged in relationships that served me. That felt like an edge to me. I knew I tended to isolate so I was wanting to expand into relationship while also maintaining a very solid focus on what was calling me.

Then I had a strange experience when I was running through my values with my base chakra last night and I read "courage" as "comfort" (How did that happen? Oh yeah, comfort used to be one of my values) and that threw my body into a very energized, reactive space. I woke up in the middle of the night after that with a very distinct call to have less comfort in my life, to consciously embrace discomfort. Was that even possible?

I seemed to choose discomfort, especially emotionally, at every turn. My lifestyle wasn't exactly uncomfortable, but it was chock full of courageous living and choices. I could feel that on some level of my energy, I was still running away from discomfort, which wasn't the same as embracing comfort. I had gotten into a pattern of cutting things short when I'd go into ceremonial space and it got uncomfortable. I was feeling like a bit of a chicken shit (oh, there was my real value being challenged -- courage). My body had been in digestive discomfort for months and yet that seemed more about spiritual discomfort.

It was time to rock and roll again into more courageous action in my life, so I decided to start pursuing getting pre-approved for a mortgage. I had never done this on my own but was trusting the call towards home, even if it didn't manifest immediately. So much of me was saying, "You need a partner to make and afford a home. You can't do this on your own." And I answered, Yeah, hi, inner critics. I hear ya. You ain't the boss of me." Onward into courageous action! At this point, I was caring part-time for my 98-year-old grandma back in my home state of NC. I was slowly not leaving there anymore, staying there more, traveling far away less often. Not that this was planned exactly – it was just what was emerging as I listened to what I wanted, stayed vigilant to my integrity, and listened for the call of purpose.

As the end of evolution 5 wrapped up, and all the coaching time with Tanja came to a close, I was still learning more and more about how integrity worked in my life. And the end of 2016, I wrote: "I had a little AHA just now. The more I obsess on something, the less in integrity I am. Another way of putting this is: when I find myself looping on something, then that is the perfect indicator of a place where I am likely out of integrity. And thus, the perfect starting place for investigation into the layer of me that needs attention, purging, expression, or what-have-you. Ahhh, life mastery."

I was at a place where I could catch the pattern or strategy in the moment and say, "AHA! I see you!"

At the end, it seemed simple enough. I make choices and experiment with options. Some work out, some don't. All provide information. If I don't keep making decisions and taking actions and going forward, I knew I'd never get to learn what was true for me. So. I was set free into the action filled life ahead of me. I was utterly prepared and confident in my skills and practices and I knew I was on the path to life mastery. All I ever really wanted throughout all the evolutions was to be master of me. And I felt I had achieved that, had arrived, had wholly done whatever it took to become the master of me.

At this time, I wrote:

"I know I'm deep into life mastery when I use my emotions to fuel a higher perspective and all the threads, the disparate aspects of my life that are slightly out of integrity, all come together woven into a new vision, into a greater understanding, into deeper awareness. I'm having a painful and incredibly ecstatic morning of listening to, seeing, accepting myself, all of my pain, all of my delight. Integrity serves. Mastery in my experience is exactly how Tanja describes it, where I scan through all the layers and levels of my being to find the aspects out of integrity and let them weave themselves back into a newer tapestry of me. It takes a little time. This most recent unraveling and reweaving has been incredibly instructive. It all makes sense and it's all kind of a ridiculous mess at the same time. What a glorious life."

Indeed.

The major changes I went through during the 5 levels? Let's see: divorce, mediations, and settlement, moving out then selling my house, moving to another town where I knew no one, passionate and doomed connections with numerous beautiful beings, my soul quest that called me back to NC after 20 years away, the decision to travel back to be with family, changing my name, the beginning of a wander that would last 1.5 years, the death of my dear canine companion after a long sickness, multiple employment changes, oh there were more.

But those are logistics, the so called "life events" that occurred during my time with group coaching with Tanja. But the inner changes, the really good stuff, the terrible beauty of falling utterly apart over and over and letting go of personas, patterns, strategies, identities, and triggers. This was the really epic stuff of the shaking loose of all of me, to eventually be reassembled into the one I walk the world as now.

All of this should be vastly apparent now at this point in this chapter. Yeah yeah, there were hardships and traumas and blah-di-blah. Ain't nothing but a thing compared to the rich and terrible journey of personal evolution. The inner journey is waaaaay more wild than the outer journey, although I had a helluva ride in my outer journey too. Thank goodness.

I discovered that the Universe really does want me to get what I wanted, if only I quit trying to control the when and how of things will look when I got it (just so, to my exact liking). I learned to surrender to how things actually end up, how they will manifest, accept the creative interpretations and hilarious impulses of reality. In other words, instead of spending so much energy pushing against what I don't want and defining how things must be, I keep my mind focused on what I do want and how I want to feel. Yes -- how I want to feel versus what the result must look like.

What were my takeaways? Well, I'm happy even, and especially, when I don't know shitola. I don't have to be wise or compassionate or empathetic or have it together or be whacked out or crazy or quiet. I know I don't have to be or do anything and yet I am everything. When I thought I had everything, it was all story and sleight of hand and artifice—a house of cards...only scaffolding was holding it up. The scaffolding had to come down and with it all the stories of who I am, why I am here, what I am to do, how I am to prove myself, what I must look like, how I must live, what it all means. When you are reduced to Nothingness and neutrality, oh the presence that begins to creep in.

We fear losing everything we have created, thinking that is who we are. We fear losing all we love and have loved, thinking that lovable makes us acceptable and thinking that love makes us whole. We are already whole. We have always been whole. Every moment has been perfect but for the garbage we have catapulted into it-- the expectations and rationalizations and wisdom spouting and wisdom seeking and self –actualization ideas and the need to be someone.

We were born someone and then we wrench ourselves into contortions to be someone else, to resemble those around us. Oh, to belong and not be alone, this drives us to distraction and effort.

Alone ain't so bad. Lonely is what we are anyways all the time. Lonely in a crowd, trying to impress and not look awkward. Lonely in relationship, trying not to act outta line, toeing the line and holding our breath so as to not lose love. All we ever think we have, we will lose. But it is really lost when it was never ours? See, this is the ultimate freedom and non-attachment, when we know that all we have is ourselves and all outside of us is a gift. We carry nothing with us truly but ourselves. We carry only what we have decided to drag around with us, which can be burden or gift.

Coaching
Donnaah

By the time I first came into Tanja's group coaching program, I was already twice-certified as a life coach, once as a Vividly Woman Embodiment Leadership Coach and once as a Live Your Genius Life Coach. I was a Reiki Master with years of training as an Advanced Energy Intuitive Healer. I had been on the path of transpersonal healing for many years. I was not looking for more training.

And yet...there was more. As always, there are spirals to be spun around and depths to plumbed again.

Being coached through High Speed Evolution is a turning-your-insides-out kind of experience but learning to coach others through High Speed Evolution requires turning your insides out with integrity and courage at the same time you are guiding others to do the same. The clients who come to me are ready and willing to do the work of huge transformation and often I and they are working through similar patterns -- different levels, different locations on the path, but walking together, journeying along at different stages, similar energies and work.

Another way to say this: we are tied together, we influence and inspire each other, we raise each other to greater levels of awareness and alignment with passion, purpose, and knowing what is. This is about getting grounded, raw, and real with each other as client and coach. I hold myself to the highest standards because I am accountable and honored to be guiding others through fears and stuckness to personal freedom and joy.

Why did I want to become a certified High Speed Evolution coach? Well, it wasn't a want or really a choice. It was a calling. I had to do this because I believe in this work. I embody this work. I have been utterly transformed by this work. I had closed my coaching business at one point and let go of all my clients. As I began this certification, I wanted to open my coaching business up again with new fire, more straight talk, and more purpose. And my coaching has been absolutely transformed by this experience.

In 3 words? Confidence, trust, knowing. I am totally confident in my coaching abilities. I trust what comes through me on the spot during sessions. I have a knowing that my clients can attest to. Information and intuition and downloads flow during my sessions.

I had been "certified" in two other coaching modalities by previous mentors. Neither of them ever listened to any of my coaching calls. The thorough certification process gave me confidence, as well as genuine feedback on my style and ability as a coach. Being witnessed and truly mentored through the process of coaching was a huge and important step for me. I came out of the experience feeling like I was truly ready to inspire others and kick butt.

I am a spectacular coach because I am a model to so many in my life already. I am courageous and devoted to truth speaking and compassionate yet fierce knowing of what is. People tell me I am wise and give me wonderful compliments, but I believe that wisdom is about saying truth. I am willing to say truth. I am willing to go the distance to represent this energetic lineage in the modern world. I absolutely want to promote huge change and transformation in the world and I know that I can do that one client at a time.

Hell, I attended every kind of embodiment, self-development program, course, workshop, etc for almost a decade. I bring all of me to this work: courage, energy, everything. All my gifts, all my experiences, these are my contributions. I take all this information and all the tools and techniques from all the modalities and trainings and have created my own program, my own mix of awesomeness.

My mission as a coach is to masterfully and soulfully assist clients to step into the kick-ass lives they know they were born to live. To courageously guide and fiercely inspire my clients to choose radical actions, based on their own deep awareness and glorious self-knowledge, that so deeply reorganize and transform their lives that they go forward as their unique, sustainable, integrated, and passionate selves, rippling their gifts out into the world and creating massive love and real connection and community.

I was in therapy for years. That was okay. It worked when all I could do was talk about stuff. I have found that action is what gets me excited, what gets things moving in my life, and coaching is all about action. As your life coach, I help guide you towards making decisions and actions that get you unstuck from your current life patterns, strategies, old beliefs, and ruts. We are all conditioned and most of us run high anxiety. This is independent of our faith, trust in God, gratitude, and intentions, although those are absolutely necessary and will be called upon deeply if/when we truly want to make changes in our lives.

I suppose the real question as you consider coaching is not "What is your plan?" but "What is your intention? Do you truly want to change your life? Not someday, but now? Starting now?" Most people say they want to change but have no real commitment to making that happen. Sounds good for a looooong time, though. Thing is, see, for a very long time I also had trust, faith, gratitude, and joy in my life. Didn't amount to creating change in my life, though.

You might be my client if you have ever said to yourself, "I know there must be something more."

I started asking myself what more there was in my early 40s in the middle of my perfect and secure life...and everything changed. I went renegade. So, there is a reason I call myself a Radical Action and Kickassery coach...because I aim to be part of your unique, bold, and courageous solution to that question. I believe in bigger, better, and more for everyone. Not just more moments of bliss and joy in your life but a life that is bliss and joy, more and more each day.

High Speed Evolution coaching is designed specifically for people ready to awaken to fearless living and wild personal freedom in body, self, and soul. I coach clients towards energy mastery using embodied practices that are available to the modern person who can't really spend their lives meditating in caves (as much as some of us would like to). I excel in helping clients create space and time in overly busy lives and design a life that fulfills them and that they won't want to run away or distract themselves from.

My style of coaching tends to be forthright, intuitive, and fierce. I tend to be very connected with the personal journeys of my clients. I've got a lot of wahoo tricks up my sleeve that will get you unstuck and moving forward in whatever area of life is currently keeping you up at night, looping through your head, or that you are trying to avoid looking directly at. I am devoted to your success and evolution.

While I am absolutely confident that my techniques create radical successes with every motivated client, there are some particular clients that I specialize in supporting:

I assist recovering goddesses and workshop junkies to get off the hamster wheel of blissful AHAs – those moments when you feel you've finally found the missing link in your journey – followed by the slow dissipation of that bliss due to lack of action and no follow though…which leads to signing up for the next shiny course, program, or retreat. I help you quit chasing yourself and take action with what you already have and be with who you already are.

I am drawn to working with aging female athletes who feel a nagging sense of dissatisfaction despite all the PBs. I support them as they discover that "something missing" in their lives: their authentic, radiant sparkle that comes from loving who they are.

I have a strong affinity for working with men who are navigating relationship and life challenges and feel like they aren't supported on their journey.

I also specialize in aligning with those who are considering non-traditional lifestyles, choices, or relationships, and those who feel like freaks, those who exist on the edges.

It's been 2 years since my divorce was finalized and, I swear to the gods, it's like I am finally waking up from a long-disturbed sleep, a wild dream of loss and wandering and emptiness and ache, except it was no dream. I lived it in every cell of my being. Everyone said it would take 2 years. I said, Pshaw. They were right. Yep, there are no shortcuts through the abyss of grief, although there have been plenty of delightful distractions and adventures and lessons interwoven with the torment and terror.

And now I am inhabiting all layers of my energies again, expanding, stretching, yawning, ready for the next iteration of Sparkledom. I have been quiet. I have rested. Now, I am feeling thrilled again, finally, to devote myself to staying on this planet for a while longer. It's been a beautiful journey of letting go of just about every damn thing for 3 years and now I am ready to manifest what is next in this wondrous experiment. Not just one eye open but wide-eyed and bushy-tailed.

Even still, I find that the more fully I embrace heartbreak, the more wholly I cry and grieve, the more joyful and accepting and uninhibited I become. My laughs keep getting louder and my smiles keep getting easier. I remember that the bittersweetness of this world is both bitter and sweet. Both tastes are savored, lingered upon, when I allow myself the full range of experiencing. So often we exist below the lowest threshold of our emotional and spiritual capacities. I aim to invite in, expand into, and feel all of the everythings. I am blessed to know the fullness of my terrible and beautiful self.

I believe it's a sign of our privilege and our comfort-seeking culture that we expect, nay demand, that things must be nice and easy and fair. Shit ain't fair, y'all. Nature ain't all nice and pretty. Hate to break it you. Harsh truths are the stuff of adulting. Absorbing grief and loss and hard lessons are the foundations of the uncomfortableness that comes with finally growing up. Then, only then, can we undertake what we are called to in this life without hope or desire for some payoff or positive result or pleasing learning experience. Then, if you persist, there arises a joyousness in the heartbreak, a snickering in the face of the futility, a respectful nod in the direction of hopelessness. Ah, it's a good place, beyond hope and dreams of better. It's called Now.

And now is where I find my sense of integrity. I often tell folks that I might just be one of the happiest people they know That's what living in integrity and insourcing will getcha. And hell of course I cry and grieve and get cranky and all itchypants. Those are necessary part of being happy. Feeling all the things and coming back to the glorious mess of life with gratitude and humility and awe.

How would I describe myself now? I am a 3 times certified life coach, wild woman trickster and wanderer, homebody caretaker of my elderly grandmother, walker of my ancestral lands, vintage trailer enthusiast, devoted to my Weimaraner companion. I intuitively follow what allures me without apology. I am a healer, coach, griever, giggler, lover of life, outdoor adventurer, and explorer of emptiness.

I masterfully guide my clients to personal freedom, creating more ease, wonder, and happiness in their lives, using my vast toolbox of renegade coaching techniques, including embodied practices, intuition, play, conscious awareness, creative fun, and whatever else I dream up in the moment. I am not afraid of a little kickassery to set them on the path to their unique flavor of personal freedom and life mastery.

And not to worry: all those renegade coaching techniques, I use them on myself, every day, continuing my own personal journey into badassery, being all of everything, designing the life I want intentionally, with space for the random collusions of Mystery and my Soul.

Currently, one thing I adore is that I have declared that I am at the end of self-development in my life. No more "all about me" energy. I am here to serve, to be of service, to give and to receive. Ultimately, I know my passion. It is to serve others as life coach, soul guide, and purpose illuminator. As you have witnessed my transformation over the past 3 years from married Seattle home owner to separated couch surfer to divorced vintage trailer nomad/wanderer, and now, to tiny house owner, you've seen me walk my walk and talk my talk. It's been a wild ride and I know it looks magical and it is. And it's not.

It's not because I actively take action to manifest what I want every day. How? I keep my nervous system clear and attuned and my emotions richly flowing. I live in integrity. I am resilient and self-resourced. I courageously align with the shifting call of my soul. I do not shrink away from my heart's griefs and joys. I trust that the Universe is supporting me. I humbly offer gratitude to my amazing capacity, to the blessings of Spirit, to those who love and support my journey, to the wild workings of Mystery. And I'm willing to absolutely surrender to divine timing. (Not without some impatience but hey I'm human and time is short in this life.) This is what I offer as a coach and guide. All of me to support all of you. I absolutely believe that you can have a magical wild life, too. If you've wanted bigger better more in your life but can't seem to get started, I'm your gal.

In the meanwhile, I am beyond thrilled with the life that is showing up for me, everything I wanted manifesting in short order in 2017. I've claimed the land of my ancestors again, settled into caring for my elderly grandmother, caring for my aging canine companion, and folding into the family dynamics from which I fled 20 years ago. I am deeply in service to many energies. I continue to expand. I laugh loudly at most everything. I cry freely at most everything. I am dancing with death mastery and emptiness and loneliness while at the same finding new tribe, community, God, Spirit, Love. I am beyond excited to make art with my 2 hands. I have so much to do, so much energy. Boom!

Join me in this declaration: I claim my life. I claim my love. I claim my body. I claim my being. I claim my ancestors. I claim my resources. I claim my vision. I claim my creativity. I claim my laughter. I claim my courage. I claim my unabashedness. I claim my freak. I claim my sovereignty. I claim all of the me and all of the everything and BRING IT ON!

I'm the One I've been Waiting For

Keli Dean

Keli

As I sit here reviewing my revolutionary evolution over the past three years on this overcast, 64-degree winter day in Austin, Texas, I am astounded at the progress that's been made. I am also struggling with the idea of letting a complete stranger into my life in ways that place me on the edge of vulnerability, so I've used my strategy of procrastination for three days! But here is the truth of the matter...I want to share this with you. I want you to know how great life can become. I want you to hear this from me - one human being to another. So, let's begin, shall we?

I'll start with the basics of my story. I grew up as an only child of a single mom. I have a half-sister somewhere that is ten years older than me, whom I've never known. I don't know my father either (that's one of the family secrets). My mom gave my half-sister up for adoption because in the 1960's it was shameful to have a baby out of wedlock. My mother knew who my biological father was, and she even told me twice, I just don't remember his name. Looking back now, I suppressed the feelings that surrounded not having a father in my life while simultaneously staying aligned with the family I did have. That suppression was likely due to obligations placed upon me by the adults in my life. I spent quite a bit of time with my grandparents who lived a few hours away.

My grandfather was an important person to me and served as a father-figure I could look up to. I enjoyed spending time with him because he let me be a kid. My grandmother, on the other hand, was an emotionally imbalanced hypochondriac and religious hypocrite. She reigned our whole family with emotional abuse in the form of shaming and blaming. We called her "the queen" not because she was honorable, but because she would metaphorically chop off your head if you disagreed or disobeyed her. She ruled with supreme guilt-tripping, then played the victim until she got what she wanted from you. She was the purest form of a narcissist that I've ever known.

My childhood wasn't all bad. I remember road-trips, summer vacations, dancing and swimming - it was all fun and enjoyable, though most of my fondest memories were when I was alone, or at least away from other family members because we were all afflicted with whatever "plague" my grandmother had given us. My mom began to make some really bad decisions for her and I during my 7th and 8th grade years. When I was a freshman in high school, I went to live with my grandparents permanently. We found out years later that my mother had brain cancer. Nonetheless, living with my grandmother was awful and I dealt with it by staying out of the house and drinking alcohol - as many teenagers do.

During those years, I endured my grandmother's terror full force. I was also raped at gunpoint by three guys I knew from school. Needless to say, I left that town the moment I graduated! Unfortunately, life didn't get better because I was still under the influence of very low self-esteem and continued to behave in ways far from being my true Self. I had no idea who I was and didn't really care to find out. I just continued to treat myself badly, like I had learned how to do in the earlier years of my life. My life was about everyone else -not me.

Time went on. I was raped a few more times while passed out drunk or after being drugged, then tried to get help by moving back "home" with my grandparents. That tactic only worked for a short period of time and until I got involved with a man who was nearly 20 years older than me. Our relationship finally ended with him almost killing me. Then another older man...and then another older (married) man. My life had become grotesque. The married man and his wife split up. I thought he was choosing me, so we moved in together. He cheated on me. I married him anyway. I thought an investment of five years was worth something, but I learned it doesn't mean anything if it means losing yourself completely. We had some good times, but the majority of our relationship was based on our emotional immaturity. After we got married, he started drinking more heavily and I joined him, sometimes just to try to connect. When that didn't work, I left...into the arms of a musician. I literally led a rock-star lifestyle for two years then went to rehab to sober up from alcohol. I was 117 pounds at that point and I am almost 5'9 tall. I drank my meals when I wasn't on shift.

Let's go back a little because somewhere in there I began my EMS (Emergency Medical Services) career. Feelings didn't interfere with my job, so I did well. I was emotionally numb. I received the "Cadet of the Year" award, amongst many other awards throughout my 12-year career. Being a leader wasn't foreign to me, though I am ashamed to say I did not lead with integrity, so I only did what I consider a decent job as a training officer and captain. When burnout came, combined with my personal life and a faltering marriage, things got worse. All I saw was the negative side of life. I got lost in the negativity while at work and even more so while off shift. After rehab, I gave up my position as a captain trying to regain my sense of self. Work wasn't as easy anymore because I was starting to

FEEL things again. I started eating healthier and taking yoga classes. I went to AA meetings regularly and worked with a sponsor. Two or three years later, after I was much more stable and clear, I quit EMS and went back to school to finish my undergrad degree in small-town USA.

The pace of that place, small-town USA, was beyond me. I got anxious because people weren't moving fast enough! Eventually, I learned how to slow down. I was meditating twice a day and that felt wonderful. My classes were going well, I had made some generally good friends and met a nice guy I was interested in whom I'll call "small-town USA guy." I continued to make straight A's but my personal life took a nosedive.

Evolution One
Keli

Your Personal Hell (actually, it's self-awareness and practices)

The first phase of my personal evolution began January of 2014. I signed up for group coaching with Tanja Diamond in order to better my sex life. I had listened to Tanja's Tantra podcast many years before, which was what attracted me to her. I absolutely love her way of making the ancient teachings accessible for those of us living in today's world.

When the group coaching began that January, I was in the final stages of completing two undergraduate degrees and was set to graduate in June of that year. I was also going through a second complicated miscarriage process, grappling with a math class I needed to complete in order to graduate, tussling with my budget on a student income and battling in the bedroom with a boyfriend who was unable to respect my needs. I was living in a state of anxiety perpetuated by the childhood emotional abuse I had endured and my former career in Emergency Medicine. Life was really hard, as it is for all of us at one time or another.

I am telling you all of this to give you a glimpse into the life I was leading at the time. I very much believed I was a victim of circumstance then, and for the next two years, too - we'll talk more about that later! Unfortunately, I am going to have to give you more of the story in order for you to see the outcome. Please bear with me while I indulge in the past for a few minutes…

I had always rushed into relationships and this one was no exception. What I liked about this guy so much was that he only had eyes for me! Since I'd never had a boyfriend like that, I jumped in way too quickly. Not long after we started having sex, we suddenly become "parents" and had some big decisions to make. We discussed all our options and decided to continue the pregnancy and move in together. I remember thinking to myself "something is off," but just continued to ignore it because I had a man who was into yoga, vegan food, and willing to love me and take care of our newly formed "family." I thought I had it made…for the first year.

Then as we journeyed into our second year together, it became way more complicated, as it does when you choose a partner for all the wrong reasons. We lost the pregnancy, went through the grieving process, then accidentally got pregnant again. Before I knew I was pregnant the second time, I was considering ending the relationship. I was a few states away at yoga teacher training when I found out although just a week before, we had a memorable phone conversation about us not being right for each other. Maybe it was a one-sided conversation, but still, we were talking about "us" in some capacity. Then everything softened with the positive pregnancy test and I called him to tell him he was going to be a daddy. We were both excited and had high hopes for this pregnancy since the last one didn't fare well.

At some point, I completely lost interest in having any kind of sexual encounter with him and read it was common for pregnant women to endure this kind of void, especially after a previous miscarriage. We opted to believe such an explanation. Then, we found out the pregnancy wasn't viable. When feelings for him didn't return, I knew the relationship wasn't viable either. The next few months were really difficult. I was still living with him, still "pregnant" because my hormones stayed elevated and my womb wouldn't release the tissue. I had sudden and embarrassing bleeding episodes a number of times, but my body kept hanging onto the tissue like I was holding onto the relationship. I lost so much blood on Valentine's day of 2014 that I had to go in for an emergency D&C and eventually had a 2-unit blood transfusion.

I stayed. I stayed for a few more months while my group coaching cohort and Tanja supported me. I stayed through all the grief and the disrespect. He continued to force himself on me because I was "his." I finally moved out with the agreement that we could still see each other but not have sex (he'd agreed to couples counseling), like starting over from the beginning.

As you can see, I was super stuck when I entered the program! I had too many commitments outside of my relationship, running high-anxiety, not expressing myself, not setting enough boundaries, being defensive when challenged or given feedback, trying to prove my worth without sex, et cetera, et cetera. My successes during this phase included doing the practices regularly, and becoming a little more vulnerable by talking about it with everyone on the forum as much as I could make myself.

Evolution Two
Keli

Breaking Patterns and More Awareness

My second evolution began in August of 2014. I was somehow still in that tumultuous relationship but that didn't last long because I found myself getting more and more depressed. This kind of depression was unusual for me and helped me to notice that I needed to make a change. I finally cut the cord in mid-August and moved very slowly back into single life.

In September, I began to report that I was noticing more changes in my life, like how I engaged with people or reacted to situations. I started to feel more clear, grounded and self-aware. My practices were becoming more regular without as much effort. Plus, I got glimpses of how emotions could move through me by recognizing, acknowledging, and allowing them. THAT was a huge thing for me because I'd been numb to my emotions for most of my life. In fact, I was emotionally constricted for so long that it felt dangerous to express myself in most ways. Eventually, and for the first time, I was able to use my voice -- Tanja called me out on a Q & A call!

In October, I quit the dance troupe I'd been running, producing, and dancing in for a couple years and reduced my hours at work to give me more time to focus on my studies. My beliefs around money began to change as we started working with our values and needs. I had no idea what those even were when Tanja initially gave us that assignment, but little by little, the clarity, understanding, and alignment came.

I continued to make myself "busy" with other responsibilities and couldn't quite stop myself from using my anxiety as a stimulant, but I was making progress nonetheless. I was at least learning to notice my anxiety by this time. And I had finally identified a number of things that had been holding me back for years: an underlying disapproval of self, inferiority complex, feelings of inadequacy, need for external validation, fear of vulnerability and embarrassment for showing my weaknesses (perfectionism). Identifying these things for myself and acknowledging them was another big step in the direction I wanted to go...towards the authentic me.

People frequently tell me they feel really comfortable around me, even when they don't know me. It was here, in Evolution Two, that I realized my facade was creating a sense of peace in others. The stoic, unemotional, controlled, neutral person I was portraying grounded other people. I wasn't mirroring anything, and that made people feel pleasant because they didn't have to look at themselves for any reason. They could just dump anything on me and I would absorb it. No wonder I felt drained and yucky most of the time.

That December, I felt my first overwhelming sense of aloneness. I didn't spend the holiday with anyone, which enabled me to feel all the grief and loss I had encountered recently and throughout my life. The Practices actually got me through it though! I had no idea that being in touch with my own emotional content could be so painful. Actually, I likely knew this on an unconscious level because I had used strategies to distract myself from feeling anything for years and years!

Since I didn't have a sexual partner, I wanted to really devote myself to self-pleasuring. This was a massive goal to take on, as I had anxiety and sexual excitement mixed-up in my brain from experiences in my childhood and adolescence. First, I began with masturbation because it was an act I tended to stay away from (I preferred partnered intercourse). I had some successes, orgasms, and crying episodes - which was weird, but the crying released something extra that provided a deep sense of calm. I threw away my vibrator and other toys to let myself know I was taking this seriously, but that didn't help.

I hadn't dealt with issues and fears of anything or anyone being near my anus, but opted to have some preventative (holistic) Ayurveda Panchakarma treatments that included oil enemas. That experience was a substantial indicator of how numb my pelvis was. I couldn't feel the oil going in and had no way of confirming for the technician if everything felt okay. A few weeks later, I started waking up in the middle of the night while experiencing orgasm. I hoped this was a sign that my sacral chakra and pelvis were waking up! Even though I believed that to be true, I entered a period of frustration and determination that waxed and waned for the next couple years. I'll tell you more about that later!

The other thing I was really aware of now was the tension in my jaw and mouth. Tanja and I figured out that it was oral-sexual abuse and that by not expressing myself (holding back my truth), it had become worse. My body was trying to protect me! Now that I was safe and had people to support me, it was time to allow that tension to fade. I started to distinguish what my own personal beliefs were and which ones I'd adopted from others. I also revisited my values and needs. I had recognition that when I don't do The Practices for two or three days, I get off-balance and confusion sets in and that if I increase The Practices when I am overwhelmed and exhausted, then I can revive myself and thrive! Towards the end of this second evolution, I posted: "I've absolutely been astounded about how quickly I allowed the emotions to move through me and did NOT allow myself to become the 'victim' (for too long).

Testimonial for the inner work that's happening. AMAZING!!!"

Evolution Three
Keli

Relating With Others and Speaking Truth

In April of 2015, I posted this when we started the next phase of our evolutionary process: "I'm extremely excited to be here with you all. This an important part of my life...including all the fears of failure, the delight in growth, and the willingness to be more vulnerable...I move towards Holistic acceptance and expression of self. LIFE IS WONDERFUL." Things were certainly on the up & up! I was doing The Practices every day and being involved on the forum fairly regularly by this time, receiving support and input from Tanja and others I had come to trust. Whoa! Did I say "trust"? Yes, I did. I had some people in my life I actually trusted. Pretty cool, if you ask me.

As a side note, in March of 2015, I decided to put myself out into the virtual dating world. I was in small town USA where no one was around that I was interested in dating. In April, I connected with a friend-of-a-friend on Facebook whom I'll refer to as "FB-guy." We began a relationship based on texting and I entered fantasyland immediately. We Skyped once, a few days after we started messaging and I became struck with the idea of someone all over again. In May, I discovered what happens when I want approval and control; I get anxious, then I get stuck in my head (looping on thoughts and analyzing) which makes me more anxious, then I avoided feelings and emotions by DOING something like surfing Facebook or organizing a bookshelf that didn't need organizing. It's was a cycle that was getting shorter because awareness had finally arrived, but nonetheless, I was still using my old escape strategies.

My anxiety seemed to increase with the awareness. I had crying fits from time to time and would frequently fall asleep during meditation or guided group relaxation exercises because of long-term sleep deprivation. I also found myself holding my breath fairly often and would consciously take a big belly breath and use other Practices to disperse the anxiety. I moved to my own place, (which I hadn't had in a few years) and purged over 500 Facebook "friends." I started sleeping in the nude because I'd never done that before without something sexual being attached to it. I eventually recognized that the diaphragmatic spasms I'd been experiencing for a few years (just prior to dating small-town USA guy) were linked to some sense of social anxiety. I never really knew I had social anxiety, but because I had become better attuned with my body throughout the program, these things were becoming noticeable.

During this phase, I lost the biggest portion of my rigidity. No, not my virginity...but I did feel like a virgin again! Letting go of control and allowing the walls to crumble left me feeling more vulnerable than I had been since I got sober. I was raw again, as if my skin wasn't on my body and all my nerves were exposed. I won't lie. It was awful for a while. But then I started getting some really clear information about some bigger patterns that were still holding me back. Are you ready for a big-reveal? Well, I understand it may not seem like a huge thing to you, but it was to me. I was finally able to witness my anxiety! I saw that I created situations in my mind which caused me to always be "waiting for the other shoe to drop." The pursuit-withdraw dynamic was so prevalent in my childhood that it had claimed me as its own. When I felt like the shoe was about to hit the floor (rejection of some kind), the critical self-talk would start by blaming myself for the perceived rejection, so I would pursue the other person in some way that would appeal to and appease them. I just kept doing The Practices instead of lying to myself that I was "preparing" for the possibilities.

As layers upon layers of old programming dropped away, I had more awareness around the anxiety and how it affected me. One particular belief I came across was equating stillness with depression. I'm not a depressed person, but when I slowed down enough, I felt like was! Anxiety was spilling over into my daily life with tears and fears and lies I told myself, future-tripping and other junk...and I was finally able to observe these things. I started taking more action in the moment to change my brain chemistry and work towards not becoming overwhelmed every time I would feel a strong emotion or hear that critical self-talk telling me I was worthless or not good enough.

My relationship with FB-guy deepened to the point that I wanted to become more vulnerable with him and share some important things, even though we had not yet met in person. The vulnerability itself compounded with his reactions to my being vulnerable created severe anxiety, so much that I had a few panic attacks. I brought all of that anxiety back to a manageable level by doing extra (preventative) Practices.

I finally met with FB-guy in December of 2015 after driving over 1,000 miles during my university holiday break. The confusion began immediately. He was annoyed with me because I didn't tell him right away (via text) that I had arrived in town, yet he didn't seem in any hurry to come see me. In fact, I think it was well over 36 hours before I actually saw him. That first date went well. He picked me up, brought me flowers, took me out for coffee, opened doors for me and even said he was excited about finally getting to spend some time together. That feeling didn't last. It was like I wasn't even in town...fifteen minutes away from his home or work. I had planned to be there for two weeks, and soon, time became torture. He kept making excuses and wouldn't commit to any plans. I felt like I was going crazy and spent a lot of time talking to Tanja, Bev (one of my dearest friends from the program), and a couple of other close friends.

The support they provided along with The Practices gave me enough courage to be able to talk to him about some of my difficult feelings surrounding his avoidance. Of course, he said all the "right" things and I soon fell back into the spell I was under. Though I actually ended up breaking a pattern, thank goodness! Even with the empty promise of meeting his two sons who were driving in from Florida, I stuck to my newly-revised, early departure date and left to spend some time with people who wanted to spend time with me in Austin. YaY Me!!!

Evolution Four
Keli

Passion and Purpose

My next evolutionary phase began in January of 2016. Warning: you'll hear a lot more about FB-guy now. I preemptively apologize! In general, he served a substantial purpose in my healing journey because so many of my difficulties were tied up in relationship stuff. I'd been super strong as a single person, as a student, and a high-performer in the workplace, but would just break down in tremendous ways when in romantic relationship (even the ones that hadn't completely solidified, as in this case).

Another enormous portion of this phase came in the form of 30-day challenges. These challenges are unique to each individual. Some people do them together and some on their own. I had never fully completed one before. I'd started a few and would get a few days in (maybe ten) them drop them like hotcakes! The first one I completed consisted of me expressing myself in some way, every day for thirty days. The second challenge was an "ice bath" challenge; and the third was no type-talking, especially with FB-guy.

The self-expression challenge started me on a path of astronomical changes. I wrote in two Facebook groups, one with my beloved tribe of reliable and compassionate people though this program and the other with my grad school cohort. Those thirty days turned my life around! It couldn't have happened any other way. You see, I had to have people in my life that I actually trusted - people I believed could be okay with the information I put out there. They also had to be honorable, so I could rest assured they would not shame me in any way. Those kinds of people arrived in my life almost simultaneously (both in 2014), then there were a couple years of trust-building, and now I felt ready to open up to them. It was the first challenge I actually completed. I think I had more devotion to Self and a clear intention from the very start, even if I didn't know what was on the other side of the challenge. I was allowing people to really know me!! I was letting the persona I had created fall away and practicing vulnerability.

On day ten of the challenge, my usual time to give-up, I got into bed that night without writing something and because I was "tired" I made a choice not to do it. Really, I was making excuses in the name of "self-care" which is bullshit when we want to create sustainable changes in our lives. I was angry with Tanja when she suggested I start over. When I got over myself, I realized I was just mad because I wouldn't be able to do things my way. Oops! Did I say that out loud?!? Yes, it's true. I'd been an anxiety-ridden control freak and perfectionist for a long time. And yes, I started over with Day One and the rest is history.

There were about six people who supported me daily on this challenge and I really felt honored to have been seen by them. I am also extremely grateful to that core group and all the others who chimed in from time to time to cheer me on! The biggest things I learned were (1) that I have something valuable to say, (2) there are people who are interested in getting to know the real me, (3) being with my emotions is okay, (4) I can allow myself to fluctuate with my emotions and still feel safe, even in the company of others, and (5) anyone who causes me confusion and anxiety isn't a person I should invest very much time or energy into building a relationship with! The fifth lesson actually comes on full-force in Evolution Five, but the seeds of it began to sprout during this challenge, hence the reason I am noting it here.

My second successful 30-day challenge was provided by Tanja because I asked her for one: thermogenic for the vagus nerve. I put my face into 40-45 degree water and breathed through a snorkel for as long as I could stand it (up to five minutes). This helped my anxiety so much! I slept more soundly and just generally felt better throughout the day. It also brought up some things that were causing anxiety for me, sometimes in the form of bothersome dreams and sometimes through awareness of bodily sensations like tension or breath-holding; I encountered many feelings including doom, dying, and loneliness (even with people around me). Sometimes I felt a sense of suffocation and learned to breathe through it until I regained my safety again. Other times waves of nausea would come over me or there would be a heart flutter. Once I battled with my critical self-talk about being a "failure" and I won!! On day seventeen, it was if my reset button got pushed and within the discomfort I felt a total sense of relaxation and calmness. I even traveled during the last few days of the challenge and it was well worth the trouble to make sure I got my ice bath each day, especially with my good friends helping me to figure out how to make it happen and supporting me through it.

Ultimately, the ice bath challenge expanded my emotional range, provided me with an inner calm that I found strength in, helped me face some of the "darker" thoughts in my psyche, and brought me a new kind of awareness to my anxiety levels...which all led me to challenge number three: no type-talking. This challenge was difficult for two primary reasons. One, my relationship with FB-guy had been built through Facebook Messenger and texting - what was I supposed to do, talk to the man? Yes!! We had actually Skyped a few times during the year or more that we'd known each other but speaking to each other was definitely not our style. Two, I had conquered the art of self-expression through writing during my first challenge and now this...it was a whole new ball game!! I took the dare and ran with it. FB-guy was even willing to "support" me through it, though he did it in his own way, of course. Since he would rarely answer his phone, I sent him video messages. He would reply by video sometimes, too. Occasionally, he would reply by text to taunt or test me, or maybe he was lazy and didn't want to be bothered, I don't know. At one point, I chose to break my challenge after he stood me up for some plans we'd made and wouldn't talk to me when I called. Actually, he answered the phone but made some weird noises (there was loud music in the background) then hung up on me. He texted me saying that he was "eating" and would call me later. He didn't. I was angry. A couple hours later I decided to break the challenge by texting him because I knew he was more inclined to respond and I needed to be heard. He responded, and I suggested we talk in person, but he wouldn't go for that. I battled my own inner critic ALL night and won! I recognized that this wasn't about who I am as a person or my worth, it was about his patterns of avoidance and shame. Either way though, my heart felt broken and shattered. I was really sad. Two days later, he came and picked me up and said all the "right" things again. Damnit! I was on the hook once more.

Eventually, I made it through the challenge in Evolution Five while coming to understand the wisdom Tanja had contributed through my difficulties with FB-guy: texting is informational, not relational. I also came to comprehend that type-talking (email, texting, writing through any kind of app, etc) does not translate to real life because we can misinterpret and project our fantasies so much easier than during face-to-face conversations.

Other successes I celebrate from Phase Four are being able to deal with disappointment easier, having better memory recall, the ability to enter into conversations much easier, and laughing much more often -- not taking life so. seriously. My emotional capacity had grown immensely.

Evolution Five
Keli

Living Courageously

I'm going to start out by saying "WoW!" This phase really brought life back into my body and soul!!! I completed three different challenges and learned so much from each one.

First was a 30-day Fire Breath Challenge. I hated fire breath. In the earlier evolutions, it had caused me pain and discomfort, but because I knew there was something in it for me, I engaged my courage and went for it. Funny thing happened - I restarted this challenge four times! The third time was on the 29th day!!! What I said on the morning of day 30 was, "...because intentions aren't actions, and distractions, excuses, & lies get in our way of progress while diminishing our self-trust ---> I will be re-starting my challenge today." By that time, I had a cheering squad and a ton of accountability, so I really felt great when I completed this one, plus my integrity had skyrocketed. I was really in touch with my own value system and was stepping into the vision that I wanted for my life. Another truly amazing victory!

The second challenge during this phase was a 10+ day ISH (internal static hold). Since I had completed a 30-day vaginal

ISH, we decided I was ready to do a lotus blossom (anus) ISH. I was now moving into deeper healing that was really scary. The first day, I dissociated. The next few days involved some crying, numbness, and basic lack of presence. Day nine was the first time I was able to relax and feel something. I extended the challenge by two days and began to have some presence in addition to a small sense of safety that came with the mindful reminder that nothing harmful was happening.

As a final challenge, I decided to do a 30-day MEGA Sexual Energy Challenge. There were many components to this challenge - seven practices, to be exact. I restarted once after leaving everything until the end of the day and being "too tired" from work to complete them. My major lesson with this challenge was that integrating the practices throughout my day helped me stay focused on what needed to come next. There is a component of creativity in sexual energy, therefore, I was gaining more focus and could accomplish more since my 2nd chakra was becoming significantly unblocked.

Oh yeah! Early on in this evolution I broke it off with FB-guy. He wouldn't answer my phone call (surprise! surprise!) so we ended it via text. Geeze. I never thought I'd be one to do that. LOL! And let me just say, I never will again.

OTHER MONUMENTAL SUCCESSES =]

(smiley face typed by my cat...impressive, huh?)

Symptoms of high-anxiety, emotional abuse, sexual assault, and PTSD were diminished....my biggest symptoms included:

Reverse breathing and holding the breath

Jaw tightness and teeth grinding

Looping thoughts and over-analyzing

Anxiety may still be present, but the care and wakefulness I cultivate through noticing, allows me to feel more at Home with mySelf. Other healing that has taken place for me over the years includes narcissistic abuse, sexual trauma, addictive behaviors, and body dysmorphia. The stuck energies of shame no longer have a hold on me either, as I can move through them with more ease. But wait - there's more. Today, I can start hard conversations even when I feel vulnerable. And my fingernails! I can grow them long and when one breaks, I don't have to chew or cut the others off. Both of these are a testament to my ownership of imperfection.

My biggest lesson has been that my body informs me. It tells when I am not living through integrity or making a wrong-for-me choice. I have experienced it's messages a number of times throughout my life - now I know what they mean. For example, the only time I've had migraines was just before my first marriage until just after my divorce was final. I also had severe GI issues as I began dating small-town USA guy. Those problems essentially went away after I broke up with him. There have been others. The most recent happened when I made a little agreement with a man about how we wanted to proceed. Unfortunately, we inadvertently placed me in the part of "the pursuer" and my psoas tightened up and pulled my hip out of place. Once I realized I was not being true to mySelf and corrected the agreement with him a week later, everything relaxed, and I could walk again. The body is amazing! It's our job to listen to it and take the best possible care of it, which isn't only physical care but emotional, psychological, and spiritual care, too.

This process isn't really an evolution, where the stresses of the environment shape you, it's an IN-volution because the work is done on the inner realms. We become insourced.

Because I wanted to help others to transmute their setbacks into something that could propel them forward and guide others to their innermost world where it's safe and calm, I decided to apply to become one of Tanja's coaches. She accepted me into the program and has mentored me since.

Coaching
Keli

To date, June 2017, I've had 12 coaching clients and over 200 hours of one-on-one sessions with them. Every one of them has been different, although I will notice themes that run concurrently from time to time.

The main lesson I've learned through coaching is that we all advance at different rates. It's important for me as an individual not to compare my successes to others, nor shall I have expectations for my clients. Where one may advance quickly through their, insecurity around food and body image, for example, it may take others much longer. There are many things that factor into the healing timeline and we have no way of knowing what that timeline looks like for anyone, including ourselves. We can certainly DO THE PRACTICES to enhance the healing process and begin to get the stored emotions unstuck, but what we do with them once they become conscious is also important - and, for me, that's the most important part of coaching someone - helping others through the stage of awareness and moving them towards "what's next."

I am inspired to work with anyone who's willing to DO the work, The Practices, and to become more of who they want to be. It may be simple stuff, but it's not easy. Anyone can have the sense of freedom they are looking for, it just takes a dash of courage, a readiness to dig in deep, and a devotion to self. And you know what lights me up? ...seeing you succeed and celebrating those successes with you!! You've got this!

Post Coaching August 21st 2017 – January 31st 2018

Remember when I told you about my psoas pulling my hip out of place because I had inadvertently become "the pursuer"? Okay. Well, please allow me to tell you more…

That man and I bonded so deeply we got scared. Honestly, it made me feel like I'd never been in love before that, and maybe I actually hadn't. Our first kiss made the walls and world around us disappear. We felt completely safe with one another and were opening up to each other in incredibly vulnerable ways. We worked through challenges with ease. The few times we were together sexually, it was as if our souls were intertwined despite our habitual ways of love-making.

He initially recognized that he wasn't ready to enter into such a bond and felt like he had to do some healing work. I believe I can do anything, so I held on...believing in "us." It became clear, in a sweet and conscious way, that neither of us were whole enough yet to handle what was being presented to us and we gently ended our private connections. It was the hardest choice to make and an even harder one to live with. We stayed connected from a distance, yet the desire within left much to be reckoned with! And the reckoning is what led me exactly where I needed to go.

Over the next five months, I grieved deeply. I cried every day. Eventually, I realized I was releasing all the losses and betrayals I'd experienced in my entire lifetime. It was he who'd given me permission to drop into a love of myself I had not been able to reach on my own. I took a rocket ship into my inner space and extracted a wide arrange of gems. I started letting go of beliefs that were holding me back from experiencing love the way I desired. Here are some of the outdated beliefs I discovered:

I am not worthy of love

Ambiguity is not okay for any length of time

Unavailable men are the issue

I have to complain and/or make demands to gain attention

I have to rely on the stimulation of anger, despair, and the pathos of hopelessness

Relying on the anticipation/excitement that somebody will love me someday serves me somehow (yeah! By distracting me from living in the moment!)

I began to focus on relationships with myself, family, and friends instead of using fantasy to keep me company and help me avoid the feeling of being unwanted. When I did so, I could see that there were a few healthy, loving relationships already around me. I started showing up for myself in more substantial ways, too. My new template formed into: "With the Universe as my lifeline, I am fully available to giving and receiving love." My intention became this: "I will no longer abandon myself, so others can abandon me more easily. I am not a victim of love and will no longer organize my life around the weakest parts of a potential partner in an attempt to prove myself worthy of their love and affection." I also ended up forgiving myself for believing that fantasy was truth, which was a strategy I'd used since I can remember my first interaction with a boy at the age of four or five.

Something really huge shifted when a man I knew during my childhood contacted me through Facebook. When I initially read the message, I went numb for a day or two (I abandoned myself again just like the last time I saw him). I couldn't pinpoint how I felt about the message, telling me how he lost his parents and offering me pictures of me and my mom. When I was able to tune back into my emotional content surrounding this person, I wrote him back: "I lost my mom in 1999. You were inappropriate with me as a child and, honestly, I want nothing to do with you."

This man was in his twenties when I was twelve and thirteen. He manipulated me into thinking he loved and cared about me. To me, he was like a big brother. To him, it seems like I was something to conquer. It was here, at such a young age that I began to relate secrets, sex, objectification, and victimhood with love. All of that, together, got wrapped into my belief system as "love" and I repeated that pattern over and over again, sadly enough recreating that abusive experience!

I'm actually glad he contacted me because it gave me a chance to dig out the pain that had been harboring itself in my psyche and body. Here is what I realized in a more expansive way:

He is the only one to blame

I am not an object

I am worthy of truth and respect

I am good enough for non-secrecy

I am no longer a victim

I have boundaries and can say "no"

I am capable of having healthy sex

I am enough

I accept myself just as I am

I can have an open heart and keep myself safe simultaneously

Truth be told, I've looked for love in ALL the WRONG places since my memory begins. It's been a long road of failure after failure and I still cringe remembering some of those scenes in my head. But even through all the physical harm, emotional pain, and relationship losses, I've never given up! You see, I believe wholeheartedly in the power of human relationship. The trick is, not relying on it/them for complete fulfillment.

I can say that I finally found the place inside of me where Love resides. Yes, self-love is important, however, when feeling overwhelmed by a sense of aloneness or a longing for a partner to share my life with, in addition to giving myself a little hug and using affirmations to remind myself that I am good enough, I can now access the ever-present Love that is innately contained within my Self.

Yes, I still want romance. Yes, I still want a deeply-bonded partnership and synchrony sex. Yes, I still want to practice all the healthy, adult ways of honoring one another though partnership that I teach my clients. Yes, I still desire a cosmic co-adventurer! A man with a huge heart who as done his own courageous work. The difference is that I am not losing myself by seeking it/him. Love is already part of me. There is no void to fill.

When the time is right...when both me and my partner-to-be are internally prepared enough to show up for one another and join together through commitment, then it will BE. Until then, I am trusting myself and the Universe to do all the amazing things It does. I am softening. I am surrendering. I am blossoming. I am living an inspired life - right here - right now - with an open heart.

The Edge of My Personal Unknown

Beverly Manchester

Bev

I was sitting in a meditation circle in a large workshop room, decorated with massive Chinese art in Lhasa Tibet. The air was thin at this altitude, making it harder for me to breathe, even sitting still. I was on a spiritual retreat, with Ger Lyons and ten other participants, in the middle of a ten-day fast. No food, only water, and a special herbal tea that was to help us acclimatize to the altitude. The workshop days were long, usually ten or more hours each day, and the work was deep. We were into day seven when Ger, sitting directly across from me, looked squarely at me, and said, "Why are you settling? Why are you settling for the life you have now, when you know there is so much more"? A surge of energy exploded like a firecracker in my body, goose bumps all over, even my hair was tingling. I saw a rose gold aura around this man extending 10 feet around him. I knew he was speaking the truth. So, it began…. "If you like Tibet", my friend Kate said, "You will love Peru".

She was leading a spiritual trip to Peru, and she was headed there soon after we would be getting home to Vancouver. When I got home from my month-long trip to Tibet and Nepal, I booked immediately for a trip to Peru two weeks later. Life seemed different when I was back home after Tibet. I was questioning my life, my decisions, my purpose, my happiness, and my marriage. I had worked hard my whole adult life. I was devoted to my family, to my husband and the shared dream of building a multi-generational farming business.

Somewhere along the way, things started falling apart. What started out to be a dream life with my soul mate that I felt unbelievable passion for, all went flat. When my middle son came to talk to me when he was age 14, my perspective changed radically. He told me he could not stand how his dad was treating me, and asked how I could put up with the daily put downs, and disrespectful comments my husband was saying to me. My son made the suggestion that I should move out, and that he would go with me and help support me. My world was shattered. I thought I was being patient, tolerant, strong, and holding the family together for the kids.

I watched my mother in the martyr role most of her life, and I thought I was past that. I did love my parents, and was grateful for much of my upbringing. I knew they did the best they could, and I knew they both had some monumental patterns and issues they could not get past. I made bold decisions to get a job, and then move out at age seventeen to go to university after I had worked part time for a year. I decided to take emotional and financial responsibility for myself. I have been self-supporting since that time.

I met my husband, Ryan, at university. For me, it was love at first sight. We were both in the faculty of agriculture. I was planning on a career as a veterinarian, and he was considering a life of dairy farming, following in the tradition of his family. I was going steady with my high school sweetheart at the time, so I put aside the strong chemistry I felt for Ryan for several years and stayed with my boyfriend. As time passed, I realized I could not be the person my boyfriend wanted me to be in the relationship, and I broke it off. This was very painful to do, and

I wish him well to this day. I knew I had to be honest, to do the right thing, and be true to myself. I had no one to ask advice from, I had been insourcing my life and decisions for some time now.

I married Ryan a few months after graduation from university, a year later. For me, it was a dream that had come true. For the first few years of my marriage, I worked incredibly hard, learning and doing all jobs on the farm that we started with his parents and some of his siblings.

The physical chemistry between Ryan and myself was intense, and I felt so much in love with him. We had three boys together. There were many difficulties in raising a family in a multi-generational closely held company. The benefits were that we were all in agreement with the business goals, and work ethic. There was some support for me to work on the farm, as my mother in law would sometimes babysit the kids during chore time in the afternoon. Most of the time, they came with me, especially for the early mornings.

The hours were brutal, and the pay was minimal. I was becoming exhausted with the duties of childcare, and working on the farm each day morning and night. Shopping, cooking, cleaning, home maintenance, car maintenance, gardening, children's activities, driving, volunteering, in addition to farm work and supporting my husband with his work was all expected. There were expectations of me as a wife as well, for daily sex. After years of this, my resources were running low. There was a church program for one morning a week that was wonderful break, and I was also able to put my oldest in a day care for two afternoons per week. That was all I could afford.

My only friend had moved away after a family tragedy and I was lonely for friendship and support. I was trying to communicate with my husband, and this was very difficult. His pattern was to stonewall, and be totally out of touch with his feelings. I remember reading an article from an advice columnist from years ago, telling a lady to ask herself the question: are you better off with him or without him? I had asked myself this question often. I wanted to make a conscious decision to be where I was. I wanted to break free from generational patterns of martyrdom, and victimhood. I told myself I was where I wanted to be. I lived with intention, integrity.

Nevertheless, life became so unbearable. My husband became obsessed with pornography. He would hide and lie about his use of materials. This had a detrimental effect on both the emotional and the physical side of our relationship. Through the years, our relationship shifted to the point where I felt he did not seem interested in me, and when he did approach me, it seemed so impersonal. I finally reached a point where I felt no connection with him, I felt used. I felt like I was not attractive to him, and that there was an underlying anger he was not expressing.

I did not understand what was happening. We tried counseling. The counselor suggested that he needed serious work on his issues, and needed to work with her on his own, but he refused to continue. I tried talking openly about what I would like to experience with him, how much I loved him, and how much his children wanted his love and attention. I tried everything to invite him into a more vulnerable and truthful space. He withdrew more and more. I continued to be married in an empty relationship for many years. I felt ignored, unloved, unattractive, and unlovable. This was eating my soul. I yearned to be seen, to be loved, and to be adored. I felt I was a giving, compassionate, hardworking, loving woman.

Nevertheless, I had this awful, insidious feeling that there was nothing I could do, nothing I could do more, nothing more I could be, to change this situation around. I felt overwhelmed and helpless. I had been working up to four jobs at a time to earn enough to support my boys in their sports, and a few extras. I was a farmer, a lifeguard, a swim coach, a strength and conditioning rehabilitation specialist in addition to being a wife and mother. Together we raised three boys, who were all active in sports.

I went back to university to earn a certificate in health and fitness. I did this out of personal interest and to help me be the best coach possible. All of these things stimulated my mind, kept me busy, kept me from facing reality. The reality was that there was no relationship left. We became housemates, co habiting as friends. I knew somehow that the inner grief and longing was having an effect on my physical health.

Over the next few years, I had several operations for gynecological issues, yet nothing was being resolved. The real problem lay deeper, and I was unable to help myself or find help through the medical system. I had picked up again on intuitive development some years earlier.

Reiki classes led me to receive initiation for Karuna Reiki master in Stonehenge. A connection from that class led me to go see John of God in Brazil. I received a miracle healing in Brazil, and I felt an immediate shift in my physical body. Doctors confirmed positive changes when I returned to Canada. I was taking charge of my health, and acting on my intuition. Many other workshops followed in shamanism, drumming, crystal work, sound healing, and much more.

These things also kept me out of the house, and learning. Travel was the next bright shiny object. "Yes, travel, that is the answer!" I said to myself. Peru was fascinating. From the first meditation the first night in Cusco, I knew I was 'home'. The trip was arranged with a great group of like-minded people, and so many interesting things to explore. Peru is a treasure box of mystery. Not just the fabulous civilization of the Incas, but many layers of sophisticated, supernatural cultures, going back further than we can imagine. Pyramids to rival Egypt, massive stone structures dwarfing Stonehenge, and whole cities built on the alignment to the stars.

I was living my life, and loving it. I had no idea what lay in store for me. Throughout the trip, Alberto, the assistant tour guide, was very attentive to me, and I was grateful, but thought nothing of it. It was pointed out to me by several people, that he had taken an interest in me. I was not there on the trip seeking male attention, nor was I looking to have an affair. I was a married woman after all, with a strong value system of beliefs.

After several weeks, I came to enjoy the attention. I started to feel something in my body. Something I had not felt for a very long time. Sexual longing. Longing for attention, intimacy. I did not believe this was possible, considering my beliefs about myself at the time. These feelings had been buried for so long. Yet, this was something I yearned for so deeply. My friend Kate and I asked Alberto to join us for dinner the last night of the tour. Kate later declined. I was very nervous. Terrified actually.

Alberto came to the hotel to pick me up. He was dressed nicely, in a sport coat and nice shirt and slacks. He is a handsome Latino man, fifteen years my junior. He took me to a pizza place close to the plaza. We ordered pizza and sangria. The warm, spicy wine went straight to my head. I was feeling good, relaxed. An easy conversation with a friend, I felt very comfortable with Alberto. I felt attractive, and I was feeling things inside of me that I had not felt for so long.

We walked to the park in the center of town, the Plaza de Armas. I was nervous, and asked if we were safe. Alberto assured me we were. I felt so attracted to him, and shy like a schoolgirl. Alberto raised my face to his, and offered a kiss. I responded tenderly, tentatively. I was kissed like I have been waiting to be kissed my whole life. Every cell in my body was vibrating, and time seemed to stand still. Life would never be the same. I went home with a different perspective.

Later that fall, I had a personal session with a healer. When he walked into the room, he looked startled. He said, "I never say this to clients, but your guides are screaming at you to leave your marriage". I was shocked. I had heard the message about not settling, had experienced a window into possibilities in Peru, and yet the inertia of being in a long-term marriage was overwhelming.

I had never thought of myself as someone who would be divorced. This did not fit in with the picture I had of my life. My parents spent their lives together, and so did my husband's parents. We were the salt of the earth kind of people. Later the next spring, I made a decision to ask for a separation. I knew I needed to live in my integrity. I could not continue with an empty marriage, while denying the fire within me. I was fighting for my life. I was exhausted. The conflict centered on my values of dedication, commitment, sacredness of marriage vows, loyalty, and steadfastness.

It came down to whether or not I would sell my soul to uphold values that did not serve me. I knew I had to do the right thing. I was no longer willing to 'settle'. I sat down with my husband, and with every ounce of energy I had, I asked him to move out, and for us to look at making a formal separation. This was the hardest single thing I have done in my life.

I said with much gratitude, and honoring what we have achieved together with our family and business, we can make this easy and gentle. He said that he had been expecting this for a while. I appreciated his calm reception of my request and had an expectation that things would proceed smoothly based on his response.

The matrimonial law in Canada is clear and fair, and I trusted the man I had spent most of my life partnered with. I ended the first serious relationship with my wealthy boyfriend based on my integrity, not greed. I was completely open to crafting a solution that we all could live with and move on with our lives. I had no idea of what was to come. No idea.

Soon after the discussion regarding separation, I was off on a trip to Egypt. This trip involved two of the shamans that I worked with in Peru, Mallku and Alanna. They are lovely people, and are friends of mine to this day. During this trip, we went to a perfume factory. The owner is a powerful Reiki healer, and had been trained in the art of essential oils – a family business for generations.

He gave aura readings for all of the participants. When he came to me, he said that I had been unhappy in my marriage for the last 7 years. He pulled me aside to talk to me privately after the readings. He said he clearly saw that Tantra is my path. He told me I must take my sexuality to the world, and that I had great work to do. I laughed because I had not enjoyed a positive sexual relationship for so many years.

He was right, however, it had been many years since I had intimacy with my husband. Before I left the store, he again pulled me aside, and gave me a present of a special perfume "Arabian Nights". A seed was planted. I started to research into Tantra. My Peruvian friends were also practicing this, and I talked with them. I was definitely interested. I bought some books, many of which I found confusing.

There were books teaching everything from Sanskrit mantras to cosmic orgasm. To me at this point, the subject of Tantra was theoretical. Many months later, I said to myself, "I need a teacher. If Tantra is truly my path, send me a teacher please." The next morning, I received an email with an invitation to a workshop put on by Parvathi Nanda Nath, a lineage Tantra teacher in the tradition of Śrī Vidyā.

I don't know how I got that invitation, as I did not know the person who sent me the invite. I signed up immediately. During that workshop, I came to respect this true master. She taught truth, common sense, energetics, mantras, and ceremonies. I could see a gold aura around her extending twenty feet on either side. She came and left the presentations in silence, and did not speak to anyone in between. I felt compelled to ask her something. I approached her, and asked her "I have been told that my path is Tantra. Do you have any advice for me regarding what you see?" She seemingly looked right through me, and responded with "yes, I see that you could be on the path of the Bhairavi (note no apostrophe here). You have very good karma to be in this class".

She later announced that this was the last class that she would be teaching, as she was going back into seclusion. There was a definite shift in my energy after that class, and I felt more drawn to this path. For the next several years I was busy with trying to move ahead on a divorce, and creating a new life. I had thought that making a business from what I love to do – travel and spiritual healing would be a good idea. I had many people encourage me to this end.

I had found my passion, and I was free! I had no idea how difficult the legal situation would become. Before I was finished, I had been to court many times, attended mediation, discoveries, and everything I could do to effect a completion, to no avail.

My spending, my personal life, my spiritual beliefs, and my value as a wife had all been called into question publicly in court. My self-worth had taken a beating, as well as my retirement savings. I called into question everything I had done and stood for in my marriage, and knew there was no turning back.

After a discovery session in preparation for court, my lawyer took me out for lunch. She told me she had never seen anyone in her career be so calm, and dignified under fire. My lawyer asked me how I did it, to remain so calm. I told her that when I looked across the table, I saw the man I married, and felt the deep love I have always had for him. I also saw his soul, and his pain. I saw how he had carried the generational patterns of his family, and was unable to put a voice to it all these years. At least in this proceeding he was finally getting in touch with his anger. I can hold space and witness him with compassion.

Holding space and not taking things personally was compassion for myself. I explained that holding space is a term used to describe the act of truly seeing, hearing and being present with a person in a neutral, supportive energetic environment.

Three years of litigation, and I was exhausted. I was finished with my last brief relationship, had a stalemate in the legal process, and had used up my savings. I was out of ideas, out of resources, and exhausted. I needed the power of the Phoenix to rise out of these ashes. I again asked the universe to bring me a teacher.

I looked online, and one name stood out for me: Tanja Diamond. She had easy to understand explanations of Tantra and its different forms on her site. I signed up for a fifteen-minute discovery meeting. I signed up for the level one Learning Tantra group that was starting within the week. I knew I was in the right place.

Evolution One
Bev

Your Life Unleashed Self-awareness and learning the practices.

Learning to have a new relationship with myself. Learning to break free from the patterns and strategies I had been using. How I relate to other people Learning to rinse and repeat. The timing of this was exceptional. I had just ended a relationship with a wonderful man. He was kind and generous with me. He offered stability, friendship, and the opportunity to create a great life together. I knew in my heart he was not 'the One' for me, and I had to be honest with him.

For as much as I enjoyed the companionship, I knew it would not be fair for him. I did love and respect him. Still, I knew with my intuition, there was someone else for him. Integrity wins again. I came into level one wanting to find love, to find the ecstatic tantric lover of my dreams and feel the incredible things I had started to tap into the last couple of years. The sexual energy was raging throughout my body. I had been told that Tantra is my path, and that I need to bring my sexuality to the world.

This is the place to be, I thought! The truth was, I had run out of ideas. I had experienced incredible spiritual and sexual events. I had been trained in many modalities, and had come to realize some special intuitive and healing gifts. I could help many people, and I could not help myself. I had to admit to myself that my life was broken. I was tired, lonely, financially in a tough spot, and saw no way out. I made the commitment to set aside what I thought I knew and be completely open. My biggest step at this level was in accepting that I was exhausted, out of ideas, and that the things I knew were not working for me. I did not want to waste time or money, and was ready to forget everything I knew to honestly try something new.

I had been having incredible spiritual experiences all my life. I depended on my intuition to guide me, and it had saved my family's life. Yet, the spiritual movement had no answers for me, only clichés. Life was getting real. Basic at this level is learning the practices - the why, and how to do essential practices of self-care. These include breathing practices, movement exercises, and getting into nature.

The nature part was easy, as I live in the country, and every time I step outside, I am in nature. The hard part was to be in nature without doing something, or looking at and thinking of all the things to do. Learning my patterns and accepting that I am programmed, and that these things are not the true me.

As much as I was aware of my family patterns of addictions, martyrdom, victimhood, and codependence, I realized I had been playing them out all my life. This was a real humbling, which led to increased compassion for my family. While listening to family and friends, I could hear the pain, the unresolved issues, the neediness, and recognize it in myself. I was no longer triggered. There was instead, recognition of what was currently being experienced.

I realized and was astonished at how long people hold onto childhood hurts and trauma. I knew that people essentially need love, affection and to be heard, and I was no different. Spiritual connection through being in nature was one of the best parts of this evolution. This practice brought me into a greater sense of myself, an expansion. I felt a slowing down, a natural patience with life, a sense of relaxation when I was sitting in the forest.

By the ocean, I learned the nature of give and take, and natural rhythms present in all life. The more I traveled and experienced nature in all its incredible expressions, the more insignificant I felt. I was noticing the microenvironment of small insects, animals, birds and how they exist in each moment driven by their instincts in harmony with each other.

A real key for me here was to practice expanding into the vastness of nature. This helped me with a clear perspective on my own problems, and stopped a pattern of contracting into myself when feeling down.

Evolution Two
Bev

Your Personal Freedom

I made commitments to myself to do the practices regularly. I wanted results fast! Teach me the sexy stuff, Tanja! Bring on the cosmic orgasm please! The fact was, that during one of the essential practices of static hold, I was feeling nothing. I was ready and excited to experience mind-blowing waves of kundalini energy. That did not happen. I felt nothing. Damn.

The sense of 'nothing' drew me in further. What am I doing wrong? My body doesn't work! I am frigid! No one will want me! Tanja help me! Tanja: "Bev, do the practices". I heard those words countless times. I kept doing the practices. Rinse and repeat. Then one day, I got it. Nothing is something. The big AHA moment! "Okay", I told myself, "accept where I am, and go deeper into the nothing". I reached stillness and a calm I have never known before. I experienced that peaceful sweet spot on the edge of my personal unknown.

The decision I made at this time was an important one. I decided to open my heart, my body, and my soul up to feeling everything. I gave up wanting to feel only what I wanted, only the 'good' stuff. To truly expand my horizons, to be Tantric, I open myself up to it all. I challenged myself to a daily practice of static hold.

In my interaction with other people, anything that had a charge to it came up during the practice. I learned how I react in my body when I am triggered. A trigger is a reaction that may be emotional or physical in nature. This led to many breakthroughs as I discovered my personal patterns and strategies, most of which were developed in my childhood.

My curiosity was aroused as more and more information flooded in. Things started to make sense, and yet I dropped the idea of making any sense at all, and chose to simply feel. I started welcoming all feelings, as this was the beginning of being grounded in my body, making my body my true home. I was finally feeling safe in my body.

Evolution Three
Bev

Your Impassioned Truth

To discover your truth, and start living in your truth. To grow confidence through integration. Recognizing the courage, it takes to live in your truth Aligning values, decisions and actions. Re training and re framing the mind and body This evolution was a big step.

It required full participation and commitment. I was doing the practices, starting to feel things, opening up to suppressed feelings and experiences. There was nowhere to hide. The online support group associated with this level was amazing as everyone is going through similar things. The online tribe and support became my refuge, my home base.

Things were getting very tough on the legal and personal front, and it seemed my whole life was being de constructed. For several years after separation, I spent a considerable amount of time in the Andes of Peru, learning from some tremendous shamans and healers. One of the many things I learned working with these amazing people, was how to accurately read coca leaves.

This is a divination technique, similar to teacup or Tarot Card readings, which I have done since I was very young. One day I asked my shaman teacher, Puma, to read my coca leaves. Puma exclaimed, "Bevy, I have never seen this!" he said. "The universe is blind folding you, they do not want you to see what is coming next. You are to live in the moment, and have faith." I did not fully understand the power of that truth in the time it was told to me.

Looking back, I know that if I had used my intuitive gifts to see what was coming, I would have avoided it as much as possible. The Universe indeed had a plan, and this plan was to have me face my personal unknown. The truth of who I am unfolded daily in front of me through doing the practices and living my life.

I was being severely tested in friendships, relationships, family, and finances. The big questions reared their head in front of me: Who am I now? I am no longer a farmer, a team coach, a wife, a mother, or a girlfriend. What is left? What is there? My deeply held beliefs were being challenged daily.

I had listed my values. These are the basis on which I made decisions. I learned that while I may have integrity as a value, not everyone does, and certainly not everyone makes his or her decisions on this basis. I had been living my life in a Pollyanna world. Nobody is bound by the same rules as I hold dear.

This leaves me to experience life as "not fair". "Yup", said Tanja, "life is not fair". Ok then! All I can do is meet life on its own terms, as I know that I cannot negotiate with life. Life always wins. The beliefs were being taken down in my soul like ancient ruins. Once great, now no longer applicable to what is happening currently. "Good things happen to good people." Maybe. Sometimes. Not always. "If I work hard enough I will get what I want." Hard work, motivation and intent are good things in and of themselves.

You may get what you want, or you may not. "Karma will make this situation right." Forget Karma. It is used in ignorance as an energetic credit card. I know if I infuse my energy with the purity of intent in line with my values, I will be current with my Karma. That is all that matters to me now, this is what will change my reality. "I deserve love." We all deserve love. Love yourself. Now. "There is someone for everyone out there. Everyone has a soul mate." "Not necessarily" says Tanja. "Damn!" I said, "I was counting on that one!" Who am I on my own? What if no one ever comes? Why waste any time at all waiting for someone? Get on with my life. See what comes.

It took me some time to expunge the deep longing from my heart. Where did this come from? Did the deep longing come from a neediness to be seen, to be loved, or to be appreciated by another person? That would be understandable from my history. Was it a deeper knowing that someone was coming to me? I went through a time of darkness on this topic.

I felt a grieving for something that I may never have, and an even deeper grief for what never was. It was the death of my dreams, of my hope and expectations. I questioned why I had gone through the hell that I have gone through just to find nothing.

Similar to what I did in evolution 2, I used the practices to go deeper into nothing, to the very edge of my personal unknown. Sitting with myself in static hold for weeks on end, crying, holding myself, being with myself, compassion grew. It was not pity. It felt like holding vigil by the bedside of a dear friend in hospice. Let it go, let it go, let it go. In trying to let go, I intuitively felt that what was needed was to not let it go, but to welcome whatever it was home.

Spending time in nature allowed me to expand my sense of self, to increase my capacity to hold space for myself. Coming out of this dark time, I knew that I was strong, very solid, and I could count on myself to never be abandoned again. My word means something. I am not alone. Everything will be okay. One day at a time. I don't have to like what is going on in my life; I only have to acknowledge what is currently happening. I was still wanting what I want – a resolution to the divorce, I wanted a deep soulful relationship and to experience cosmic sex. I knew that these desires kept me out of being present. I also knew that I could not ignore them.

I intensified my practices. Self-care, self-pleasure, breathing and static hold was now being done throughout the day. I was challenging myself to thirty-day practice challenges. I was learning to be there for myself, to trust my own word. I was starting to feel in my body. Surges of energy followed by waves of whole body orgasms, sometimes lasting for hours. I was giving myself permission to open up to myself and not expect the ultimate sexual experiences to come from an outside source. I realized in all of the incredible fourth level sexual experiences that I have had, I was the common denominator. It was during this evolution that my nightmares stopped.

Nightmares that I have had since I was a teenager. On a deep somatic level, things were being worked out. I did not need to know everything that was going on, all I needed to do was to trust the practices to do their magic. This was building my confidence, and building much needed reserves.

During this time, Tanja held a women's retreat. I went and met some others from our group, and from the USA and Canada. The location was stunning, on the beach on Whidbey Island. I felt safe to open up, and felt respectful of others when they did as well. I was amazed at how Tanja could bring out so much of people, at how vulnerable and present she was herself. During one exercise, Tanja and I looked into each other's eyes. She started to cry. I was experiencing a vastness of space and stars in her eyes. I have never felt so seen in my life. I knew I had truly met an old cosmic friend.

Evolution Four
Bev

Your Awakened Passion and Purpose

- Purpose is self-management, self–care

- Passion arises from self-care

- Action – daily courageous action

Key point – we have choices. When we don't want to make decisions, it is because we are scared, or it doesn't fit in with our values. I now understood that making no decision is a decision. I started breaking through patterns of procrastination, denial, evasion, and distraction, through daily action.

The actions I took were supportive of myself, no matter how small. For example, choosing to shop for and make the best, healthiest food. I exercised daily, and rested when my body said so. I invested in health care practitioners who had the skills to rebuild this body and relieve pain. The littlest things matter, even on a very tight budget, you can take simple positive steps. It is the message you send to your body and soul that matters. That you matter.

Coming back to self. The rest of it doesn't matter. This was a tough lesson, and I soon learned to enjoy it. Giving myself the attention I always wanted. Passion comes from the action of caring for yourself. A lesson well received. I have learned that caring for myself is a full-time job!

Near the end of this evolution, I had a final resolution to my relationship ending in divorce. It had taken six years, three lawyers, and every resource I had. It was worth it. This evolution was essential for me to realize that self-care is the basis of what I do. No one is obligated to take care of me or love me. That is my job. I feel grateful and complete with that chapter in my life, and all who participated.

I learned to refine my values and needs. I listed my resources and started to build my team. Team Bev. I have started to pull together resources of teachers like Tanja; new friends like my fellow coaches, professionals that I respect for financial and legal advice, body care workers. I have changed my look, my health, my attitude, and my life. This evolution was about putting all that I have learned into daily practice. The practice of living an authentic life, one I could be proud of.

Evolution Five
Bev

Your Courageous Action

- Taking courageous action again and again

- Living in integrity

- Living how it honors yourself first is courageous

- Have the courage to know few people will ever live this way

- Understand the importance of tribe

I found it essential to belong to a tribe that 'gets' me. This is important because few people truly live this way – living their truth with integrity, and making courageous decisions based on their values. I started listening to people in a new way. It became clear how people chose to be stuck in their lives. People were telling me the same stories year after year with no action being taken.

I became a very good listener. I was now listening with clarity and compassion. I respected people wherever they were at. The last thing I wanted to do was offer unwanted advice, throw some clichés at them, or be so arrogant that I could not see myself in their shoes at some point. People have always approached me, and opened up to me, wherever I am. I gained a new respect for the term 'holding space' for someone to express themselves. It is an honor to do so.

Dealing with loneliness – this was big for me. I learned that even if I am not partnered, it is very important to have a tribe. Even with a partner, I may be lonely. I knew that from my marriage.

Living life in integrity is a courageous action. For me, integrity means being in alignment with all my values and needs, being aware of my patterns and strategies, making bold choices to stay true to myself and holding myself accountable. These are lofty ideals indeed.

I am reminded of how there is nothing so inspiring as the first few hours of a diet. A short-term diet, however, does not make a healthy life. A commitment to a healthy lifestyle where I naturally include healthy choices and behaviors that support me does make for a healthy life. It is similar to what I have learned here. It is the conscious integration of all that I have learned here that make the choices sustainable.

It is easy to get tripped up trying to stay in integrity. Some of my patterns surround belonging, being loved, and the need for touch. People naturally want to belong, and many of us will compromise our integrity to get our needs met.

This evolution is not about getting what you want. A big part of it is developing sustainable courage, will. This will take you far; keep you on track with integrity.

For me, this evolution is also about accountability. Am I really walking my talk? What do I do and say when no one is watching? How do I compromise myself?

A good case in point on this is my weak spot of relationship, love and sex. I have had a friendship with a man that I had had exceptional chemistry with. He regularly sent me invitations to visit him when he is in between relationships himself. We get along well as friends, like the same activities, have inspiring conversations, are both talented healers, and the sparks fly physically. So, what is the problem you say?

He has told me that he is looking for a relationship with a younger woman. To go and be with this man has torn me apart. Despite loving to be with him and share with him, every time I look in his eyes, I feel the hurt of his words in my heart. I know to truly stand in my integrity; I cannot allow myself to go there. The physical aspect, and the lure of a close but not quite relationship may have fooled me in the past. I may have deluded myself, or told myself it doesn't matter. The age difference does not matter to me, as I have dated younger men than him, but it does to him, and I feel judged by it. I have visited him, and had wonderful experiences with him. I knew I could open myself absolutely fully to this man, and let it stand at that. I was not attaching to the experience or wanting more in terms of commitment. I loved him, and yet I did not want a relationship with him.

Self-care is making the best decisions to protect my confidence. I cannot go. I know now what I am capable of in intimate relationships. I open my heart completely. I can read the soul of my lover, and have the energy mastery to take us to heaven. I would like to find a partner with similar capabilities to share with me. Having love and compassion for myself means to not put myself in situations where I am settling, or made to feel less than.

I have accepted the responsibility for my actions during my marriage. I see now how I compromised myself to stay married, thinking I was negotiating in good faith. I ended up giving far too much of myself away, draining myself. Big lessons in boundaries have been learned since then, and have been a revolution in how I deal with friends and family now. With this clarity and compassion for others and myself, I have seen relationships shift and some fall away. Everything is working out. Every choice I make in line with my values I feel in my body, strengthening the energetic core and each body wisdom center.

I know there are no guarantees in life, I can only give myself the best chance to be successful, happy, healthy, and accept the responsibility for the choices along the way. There is little energy lost now in shame or blame. The most amazing life has texture, not perfection. It is how I deal with the ups and downs, everything that comes my way that creates my personal history. I have learned by accepting all feelings, from the first evolution, this process is opening the door to a much richer experience. It is this way in the larger context of accepting all that life presents. The good, the bad, and the ugly all have their gifts. I am not white washing here. Some experiences are downright awful, and I acknowledge that. The gift for me is in being real, honest, and present to what is currently happening. There does not have to be a lesson or higher meaning-sometimes that could be a pattern of spiritual escape also.

A big side effect of living at this stage of evolution is the cessation of worry. The decrease in anxiety specifically is how I finally started to sleep at night. I don't have to work on something all the time. I don't need to constantly look for the next thing to heal or let go. I found that just creates a looping dynamic of its own. Therefore, I have let go of healing my life in preference for living it. I am grateful to have the chance to live it!

I am noticing I am resting more, sleeping more, catching myself up on self-care. Not just vanity care, but going for walks, doing yoga, eating well, taking a nap, listening to music, catching up with friends. These things are not distractions from things I don't want to do. I am integrating them into my life. I am more energized in my activities, and more positive in my outlook.

So, what is the next step for me? I am re-creating my life in every aspect. I will have to move from the family home I have lived in for over thirty years, this year. I will need to find a new home, support myself with a job, I would love a relationship, and I need to look after my health. Where do I start? The logical place to start is what inspires me.

Coaching
Bev

I started on the Evolution Coaching program in the last year, initiated by Tanja Diamond's invitation. This was intensive training, and really held me accountable to what I have been saying and living. With my past experience as an athletic coach, I knew I had certain skills to offer in the coaching area, and that I felt energized and felt I was living a life of purpose when working with clients. This was a good place to start. Start with what I know.

The clarity offered by what I know I have to do, and with what I like to do started to put some pieces together for me. The encouragement from Tanja, and the other coaches was instrumental in helping me along. I had some great clients in my practicum, and I am so grateful for their faith and trust in me to guide them.

I could not be prouder of their progress, and evolutions in their own lives. Some successful results are life altering, and some results are subtle. I have also noted that success does not just come from the awareness of my clients. It is the mark of a great coach to get the client to take the next step into action. Then to repeat the steps into consistent action that creates true lasting change. This program is about empowering people, and teaching them skills that they will use for a lifetime.

Life Mastery is not about having the perfect life. It is not about getting everything you want. It is more about being able to figure out what is not working, what to do, and being ok with not getting everything you think you want. Life is not always fair. We have to be real, and know that we will be OK, no matter what comes.

The true gift of this program is that I now know what integrity feels like in my body. I know how to insource, and resource myself. I know my values and needs, and what drives them. I have more compassion for myself, and others.

Finally, I am inspired and extremely excited to offer this guidance and information to others. If you feel powerless over your body, life or choices; if you feel you are at a crossroad in your life; if you are ready to commit to yourself, make courageous decisions and take bold actions; this program is for you. I look forward to working with you.

February 4, 2018

Update from Bev:

Almost a year out from writing, and I can report I am more confident in who I am and where I am going in life. I have been living my passion and purpose, with my heart and mind equaling guiding me in this exciting adventure. There is great clarity in how I see the world, and my place in it. A high level of self-care has supported me to enjoy superb health and vitality. I enjoy walks in nature, yoga, swimming and travel.

I still do my practices, and they have become second nature, integrated throughout my day. In one breath, I can ground myself and change my state to a level of calm that has become my signature. I have moved out of the family home and completed all aspects of my divorce. I enjoy great relationships with my sons and their families. In particular, I have put in a great deal of effort to respect my own and others' boundaries, leading to a new level of healthy relationships in my life with both friends and family.

There has been more space opened up in my life for coaching clients, which I love.

I have managed my finances well, bought my own home, and am able to live overseas for part of the year.

My greatest joy has been in sharing a beautifully intimate heart space with my loving partner.

Yes, indeed, dreams may come true.

My Journey to Personal Freedom

Changing Patterns Breaking Free

Robyn Streiner

Robyn

Hi there and welcome!!! It is my pleasure to share with you in this chapter my story and journey with the High Speed Evolution program but first I need to tell you a little about myself, otherwise you will not be able to connect with me as a person and to understand where I came from and why I am here.

WHO AM I?

Well, that's a huge question in itself but in a nutshell, I am a 57-year-old happily married woman who lives on the Sunshine Coast in Queensland, Australia. I have three children, two delightful daughters who are both married and have children of their own, giving me three beautiful granddaughters. My two daughters and their husbands both live and work on the Sunshine Coast. My son, is the baby of the family but I guess at 26 years of age he would shudder at the thought of me calling him my baby!! He lives with his lovely girlfriend about an hour away.

I have been married for 34 years now to the love of my life, my wonderful husband Rick. Together, we run an amusement machine company, operating coin-operated entertainment machines like pool tables, jukeboxes, pinball and chocolate machines. In addition to this, we have a jukebox party hire company and we also provide ATM machines to resorts, Clubs and shops.

In our lives prior to moving to the Sunshine Coast, Rick ran a very successful Pro Shop at the Forbes Golf Club for 13 years where he was the resident Golf Professional. Over the years, my very clever husband grew this business to be the largest golf supplier west of the Blue Mountains, he ran TV commercials, had a travelling Golf Shop servicing small, remote golf Clubs in the far west of the State and also developed a Dial-A-Quote phone line where golfers could ring for a quote and the goods would be shipped direct to their door from the manufacturer. This was a very clever and innovative marketing idea considering this was in 1990.

While he was busy building his empire, I was teaching Business Communication at the local TAFE (Tertiary and Further Education College), then typing at the Catholic Boarding College before having the three children. Post-children, I was offered part-time work teaching at the local Primary School which I loved and continued to do up until we left Forbes in 1994.

I would say my life is just about as good as it gets but I am happy to say that I have made it that way and I believe that anyone can have the life they choose to live.

MY BACKGROUND

I was born the youngest of five children and have three brothers including a set of non-identical twins and one sister who is the eldest in the family and 12 years older than me.

My Dad was in the RAAF (Royal Australian Air Force) and so we moved around a fair bit when I was younger which I thought, at the time, was very exciting!! Maybe this is where my love of travel and adventure comes from. We were even lucky enough to live overseas in Malaysia for a little over two years when I was ten years old. I did not know at the time, but my Mum and Dad chose to do this to get ahead financially as they were paid quite good bonuses to live overseas. It's quite amazing to hear these stories as an adult and to understand the choices that were made and the impact they had on your life. As a child, all I saw was adventure………….

Being a military man, my Dad was also a very strong disciplinarian. We didn't get away with too much as children and if we did the "wrong thing" we would certainly know about it with a swift slap across the backside. We were taught to have good manners and to be kind to others and we were always surrounded by a very loving environment. My Mum was a stay-at-home Mum and I have memories of coming home from school with all my friends in tow to devour my Mum's cookies or whatever else she had baked on that day. She always welcomed my friends and my brothers' friends and there was always enough for everyone. It was a busy and often noisy household filled with lots of people and lots of laughter.

I used to wonder how my family managed to always have enough but then I see my Mum who, at the ripe old age of 92, still knows where every cent is spent. She always tells the story that Dad used to be in charge of the money, as it was considered the "man's role in those days" until one day a debt collector knocked on the door and wanted to take Mum's washing machine.

She was horrified when she found out that Dad had forgotten to pay the installment that was due to be paid. They sat down and talked about how awful that had felt for both of them and decided that if Dad was responsible for making the money, it was going to be Mum's responsibility to make it go around. They were married for 68 years and Mum paid all the bills, never once being late with a payment and Dad received his weekly pocket money, he used to call it, to spend in whatever way he chose.

I see now how we as children learn so much from our parents and we often take on their patterns or ways of doing things well into our adulthood. Some of these patterns are great modelling experiences and unfortunately some of them are not. It is only when we are adults and look at our own behaviour that we get to decipher which patterns are truly ours and which are our parents. Lucky for us, that everything in life is a choice and we get to make it for ourselves!!

My sister, who I mentioned is 12 years older than me, was married at the age of 18, so I was only six years old when she left home, so I always felt like I never really had the chance to get close to her. Still, today we are not really very close, she is a very different person to me in so many ways and although we see each other often and share the responsibilities of looking after our aging mother, I would consider some of my closest friends more like a sister to me.

My eldest brother and I are the closest as I think our personalities and the way we live our lives are very similar. He reminds me so much of my Dad and is as "soft as a marshmallow" underneath the strong and bold exterior. My twin brothers are as different as chalk and cheese, both in looks and personalities. Both of them have lovely families and although they live in a different state to me, we are always in each other's thoughts and have constant contact with them.

I love and adore my family and so it was no surprise when, during Level One of the High Speed Evolution course, Tanja gave us the task of choosing our top 6 values in our life, that family was my number one.

My memories of my childhood are very happy ones, moving town every time my Dad had a move with the RAAF, the first one when I was four years old, then at the age of six, overseas at ten, again at twelve and then when I was fourteen my Mum put her foot down and said no more moves, so my Dad retired from the RAAF and worked as an assistant in a local primary school until he retired, over thirty years ago.

I remember not ever having too much money, my Mum made all our clothes because we couldn't afford to buy them from the shops and my Dad at one stage had three jobs to make ends meet. He did his military job during the day, drove school buses in the afternoon and then did a few shifts a week as a barman in the local hotel. We always had fun playing hopscotch and ball games with other kids in the street, and I remember climbing trees, going fishing and swimming at the beach.

Every year for six weeks over our Christmas school holidays, we would pack up the car with the tent and everything we needed, and we would all pile into our little car and drive all the way to the Queensland / New South Wales border to stay by the beach. It was probably only a few hours' drive but felt like an eternity!!! We had rooms in our tent, a kitchen area, bedrooms and Dad even put carpet on the floor. We stayed in the same caravan park every year and Dad would drive back home to work during the week and stay with us on the weekends, when he didn't have holiday leave. I know now, that was all we could afford but at the time I loved that tent and those holidays.

Interestingly enough, my husband has never been camping in his life and to this day we have never been camping together. We took our kids to stay in some cabins once and told them that was camping as all their friends went camping and they felt like they were missing out. The night we went there was a huge storm and our friends in the tents were drenched and their tents destroyed and ended up at our cabins for the night. My three children have never really become campers preferring to stay under "five stars" instead.

WHEN DID MY JOURNEY REALLY BEGIN?

I met my husband at the age of 22 and fell in love on that same night. It was a random introduction by my cousin, who had been to school with my husband's sister and we were in the local golf club having a drink. My cousin wanted me to meet the local police detectives as it was their "hang out" but my husband, who was the trainee golf professional at the club happened to be wandering through.

I remember the shirt he was wearing, it had a bird on it and that blonde hair was just breathtaking. We instantly talked, he bought me a drink, we had a dance and apparently (this is the story he tells our children) that I asked him how many children he wanted to have and then I planted a kiss on his lips while we were on the dance floor.

The next morning, my Aunty, who we were visiting at the time asked me how our night was, and I announced to my whole family that I had met the man I was going to marry. We were engaged less than three months later and moved interstate together when my husband accepted a job as Golf Professional in a small country town called Forbes.

Rick and I moved to Forbes together, at which time we were engaged and were married within twelve months. Our three children were then born over the next few years and our family life began. Just like many young married couples, we had our ups and downs, it is a difficult time when you are wealth-building and creating a family simultaneously.

Our shop was open seven days a week, and as the only professional within hundreds of kilometers, Rick was extremely busy...... giving lessons, running the shop, making sure the Committee of the Club were happy and generally trying to build the business. I was totally absorbed in raising the children and had no family nearby to help. I remember constantly whining that Rick worked too hard and was never at home to help but in hindsight I realise that he was focused on his own agenda and doing all of it for the family!

We had an incredible social life, as is often the case in the country, making the most of every opportunity to socialize and trying to have a little bit of "couple time" whenever we could. I found our relationship very fulfilling except for the fact that my libido had seemed to leave me when I became a Mum. I was tired looking after the three kids and so my desire for sex and intimacy was not very high on my priority list. Rick, on the other hand, was always very highly sexed and I often felt a huge pressure to perform just to make him happy. You can imagine how this escalated over time and I even remember a conversation I had with my girlfriend and also ultimately with Rick too, stating that I didn't like sex! There was a wedge being driven between us even though in every other aspect of our lives we were totally happy, we were totally failing in the bedroom, well really, I was.

I was floundering knowing that I really didn't enjoy sex, it became a chore and I am certain it was not at all pleasurable for Rick in these circumstances either. He had a wife that he loved, his soul-mate, three beautiful children and yet he was not satisfied in the bedroom. As a Golf Professional, he was highly regarded by many people in the community and had many advances from women who thought it would be a feather in their cap to "bed the Golf Pro". He has told me that there were many occasions when women threw themselves at him and begged him to sleep with them, but he loved me and knew that he wouldn't do that to me. A few more years followed in this manner until Rick decided that it was going to be a very long and unhappy life if his sexual desires were not being met by his wife. One night he packed a bag and left and said he couldn't handle it anymore.

What an absolute shock!!!!! My husband who I loved and adored had walked out the door. How did I feel????? I was absolutely devastated, a crying, blubbering mess thinking about how my life would be without him. It was like my heart had cracked open in my chest and I was dying from the pain. On that night, I realised that I had to change, that I had totally taken on the role of Mum and neglected my other hat, wife and lover.

I rang Rick and begged him to come home, which he did the very next day. There was a lot to sort out and talk about but neither of us wanted to live without the other.

Over the following years we continued to give our relationship as much priority as our often-demanding lives would allow, we were happy, the children were now starting school and business was flourishing. I distinctly remember one statement that Rick made which was a game changer for me and the way I felt about having sex. He said to me that when he wants to make love it is his way of communicating that he loves me, as he feels his closest to me during that time. For him, as a man, he needed to feel close to feel fulfilled and making love did that for him. It suddenly melted something in me, as I now felt that it was not a chore and Rick wasn't being demanding or needy, in fact it was the total opposite, it was an absolute expression of the incredible amount of love he had for me. When I think back to those times now I realise that having a great, fulfilling life is all about choices. At the time, I was not into personal development, computers were just starting to be introduced, so access to online self-help was not available. What I had was girlfriends to talk and share stories with and we relied heavily on each other for support, both emotionally and physically with tasks like child-minding and school drop-offs and pick-ups. These girls were my tribe, and one of my greatest resources at the time. I have such great memories of our life in the country, they were the struggle years in so many ways and so it is no surprise now that my keen interest is to work with young Mums and couples who are experiencing the exact same issues that I did almost thirty years ago. My mission to help couples stay together (if that is what they both choose) and to reduce the divorce rate is a very strong burning desire because I know that there is no need to struggle so hard if you have the tools to help you understand yourself, your patterns and strategies. I didn't have the tools, but I still made it and so imagine how incredible it would be to give these tools to young couples and help them avoid struggling so hard.

LEAVING THE COMFORT OF SECURE JOBS AND A GREAT BUSINESS

My family lived in Newcastle and my husband's family lived in Queensland at this time and every holiday I would pack up the three kids and drive the seven hours to Newcastle to stay with my Mum while Rick worked. We went to Queensland once a year as a family to visit his parents and I remember very clearly driving home after one holiday in tears. Not only was I sad leaving the family but I loved being near the beach in the beautiful warm weather and really envied the healthy, outdoorsy lifestyle that Queensland represented. I knew that Rick was getting tired of working virtually seven days a week, dawn to dusk with very little time off. What was the answer??? Is this what our life was going to look like??? What are the job prospects going to be like for our children???? Is there any future for us in the country???? What else could we do????

The next time we visited Queensland we decided to take a leap of faith and purchase a small house which we could rent out with a vision that someday in the future we could move to the Sunshine Coast. We wanted to own a piece of this beautiful place, that way we had a vision that our future would be different in some way. We were both very happy and on our next visit to Queensland, quite a few months later, to inspect the almost completed house that we were purchasing, our lives changed completely. The agents who sold us the house were business brokers as well and asked us why we didn't just move to Queensland??? Sounded like a very simple question but we had a huge business and I had a job, the children were at school, we were very firmly entrenched in the country, even though we knew that we didn't want to stay there forever.

The agent said, what have you got to lose, you have a few days left in Queensland, come and have a look at some businesses with us. We looked at each other and agreed to humour them by going along to look at some businesses, we were also very curious. We looked at ice cream shops both on the beach in Noosa and in Mooloolaba and a Cookie Man franchise in one of the shopping centres. One thing Rick had firmly in his mind after 13 years in the Golf Shop was that he was never going to work in retail again!! He wanted a lifestyle and did not want to have to be at other people's beck and call, to have freedom to do what he wanted when he wanted and to earn a good income. Well, the old saying be careful what you ask for suddenly came true as the agent then told us about a business he had in his bottom drawer as he was unsure how to market it to others and was also considering possibly purchasing it himself. It was a cash business that had amusement machines like pool tables and arcade games in many different locations on the Coast.

The owner of the business wanted to open a Camping Store with his son so was selling it to give him the capital to open his new business. We agreed to meet with the Owner and the Agent the next day to look at some of the sites that the business owned and to tag along for the day to see what was involved.

The very next day we did just that and as the day went on I think we both realised that we had found what we were looking for. This is how we could make the move from the country and have a lifestyle business that gave us freedom to work when we needed to and have down time when we wanted to. How could we make this happen??? We had to be on a plane the next day??? We couldn't make such a huge decision right there on the spot, could we??? We decided to buy the business right there and then, but we had a five-day cooling off period which enabled us to check the figures both of the business we were buying and whether or not we could afford to do this. I remember sitting on the plane on the way home and looking at Rick and we were both in shock.

What had we done? I think we talked all the way home (very quietly because our children were way too young to keep a secret and we couldn't tell anyone until we had made a firm decision). We have always been in sync with our thoughts and Rick and I both agreed that we never ever wanted to die wondering or ever say what if. The figures looked good, the Owner of the business agreed to stay on and work the business for us for six months so that we could sell down our house, the business stock and organize this huge move. A Golf Professional in Australia cannot sell his business or any goodwill as it is attached to the Golf Club and is handed to the incoming professional. We were walking away from 13 years of blood, sweat and tears, a highly successful Dial-a-Quote campaign to take up a business in a different state that we knew absolutely nothing about!!! We did do the worst-case scenario talks and concluded that if it all went pear-shaped Rick was still a Golf Professional and could get a job teaching and I was a Primary teacher so also had the capacity to work, we would have lost everything financially but we would be living in the most beautiful place in Australia, we were close to family and we had each other, we would be ok.

So, six months later, after a week of farewell parties from all our friends and everyone we had been associated with over the past 13 years we drove in a convoy, Rick in the Pantec truck packed up with some leftover stock and the children and myself in our Holden Jackaroo and we made the long road trip to Queensland. We arrived at our little house in Maroochydore on Dec 21st, 1994 and had the most wonderful first Christmas here on the Coast with a cute little Christmas tree on our coffee table and a house filled with boxes, it was chaos but I remember feeling very happy.

We still have the same business today and it has changed and grown with different technologies that have been introduced into entertainment equipment but to this day we still enjoy that lifestyle business that we "asked for" all those years ago.

Looking back now I realise how gutsy a move it was but we had faith in our abilities to make it work and we followed our heart's desires to have more time with our precious families and more time to enjoy life. Many people would call it a leap of faith, I call it trust and faith in ourselves and each other and following our instincts or intuition.

WHEN AND HOW DID MY SELF-DEVELOPMENT JOURNEY BEGIN?

I was really happy with the move we had made, and life went along very nicely, business was growing, Rick was learning very quickly about electronics and becoming quite the expert at fixing any problems we had with our machines. I took up some part time teaching contracts while our children were at school and we were all involved in our own leisure or sporting activities, so life just seemed to be cruising and the years just ticked over. There were the usual ups and downs of life (a few stitches and broken bones, boyfriends, heartbreak, drunk teenagers) but nothing that was too big or too hard to overcome together.

When the girls left home, our first daughter travelling overseas at the age of 17 and then our second daughter going to University in Brisbane the year later, my life changed. Our son was still at home but, as a 16-year-old teenager, he was busy with his own life, still at school but pursuing his love of music through his new hobby of DJ-ing and looking at ways of perhaps starting his own on-line business, he certainly was a chip off the old block!!

I now had time to think about me!!!! The prospect of my role of Mum coming to an end was both scary and exciting but scarier than anything. I had thrown myself so heavily into the role of Mum that it had really been my everything for all those years. What would I do now?? What did I want to do now??? Around the same time my friend asked me to come along to a workshop with her that was being run by a woman who also ran a meditation group and here is where my life totally changes.

The workshop and meditation group were the beginning of the journey for me, I had never really questioned why I behaved in a certain way before, or considered what triggered and upset me and why when I was upset that I would retreat and internalise my thoughts and feelings. I had never done any meditation or spiritual kind of things in my life, my family was religious, so I went to Church and Sunday School. All of a sudden, I questioned everything!!! I was 45 years old, and I jumped into a totally new way of thinking about the world. I examined all my thoughts and feelings, I questioned why I never actually said what I really thought, I bought Angel cards, I had clairvoyant readings, I went to retreats where people swam naked and were vegetarian and I even changed the way I dressed, preferring flowy hippie-style skirts and tops. As you can imagine, my family was turned upside down. Who was this woman and where was their mother??

I remember my eldest daughter telling me she hated me and that I was in a cult and I had become selfish because all they ever heard me saying was "It's all about me". My husband kept asking me what I was doing, he also thought I was in a cult as I was acting so differently.

I remember saying to my husband that he had to just trust me, that this felt right for me and that everything would work out. He asked me why I wasn't happy, but I told him on many occasions that I was and that was the truth. I was 95% happy but there was that 5% that was missing, and I didn't know what it was or how I could fulfil it. I was starting to find out that I didn't really know myself and the simple Hawaiian philosophies that I was learning made sense to me. I loved and hated going to meditation for as much as it felt good on most occasions it kept presenting questions for me over and over again. I now know that it wasn't only the meditation and changing ideas that was presenting issues, that there was some internal tension in the group and that was causing problems for everyone.

The Hawaiian philosophies that I learnt were written by Serge Kahili King and still resonate with me to this day. In fact, in my coaching and massage room I have a beautiful print of them on my wall and I actually chant them before I begin a Lomi Lomi Massage. Yes, Lomi Lomi massage was one of the many things

I studied after my children all left home. My love of learning kicked in again for me after I stopped the hands-on mother role and I am still learning, in fact, curiosity is one of my six top values in life.

Just for your information and because I love to share my knowledge the Seven Principles of Huna are:

Ike- The World is What You Think It Is

Kala- There are no Limits

Makia- Energy Flows Where Attention Goes

Manawa- Now Is the Moment of Power

Aloha- To love is to be Happy With

Mana- All power comes from Within

Pono- Effectiveness is the Measure of Truth

During the few years I went to meditation I also re-kindled my love of singing. I had been in a choir for a few years but now I also started writing my own little songs that the group could sing too, it was fun. Coupled with some internal conflict and the fact that the lady leading the group consistently travelled to Hawaii the meditation group came to an end and I started looking for something else to continue this quest for learning and change.

I was sent an invitation to a one-day workshop for women to be held in Brisbane about Tantra and how to love yourself, basically love the skin you are in and how to nurture the feminine. This had great appeal to me, so I gathered a few friends and off we went for the day. Wow, that was another experience that changed my life and its direction. We did breast massage on ourselves in front of all the other women and talked very openly about sexuality and relationships. My libido had steadily been on the increase after my massage studies as I found that massaging had heightened my sense of touch and the sensuality of the Lomi Lomi massages that I was also receiving were awakening a sexuality, softness and desire in me that I had not felt before. I went searching for more courses as this felt like a great avenue to pursue, so I found a Neo Tantra course being held in Byron Bay for a week. By now, my husband was beginning to see that I was changing in a good way and so he held on tight and rode the rollercoaster for a bit longer as he was feeling very fulfilled in our relationship, but still a little uneasy at all the "woo woo" as he called it.

The Neo-Tantra was, of course, all about sex and while I found it a fascinating week, learnt a lot and met some lovely people it was not exactly what I though Tantra would be. I started to do more online research, and this is where I first came across Tanja Diamond. Here was a woman who had studied Neo-Tantra, worked with Masters and done all sorts of other training in her life and then decided to put it all together to form something that would fit with modern life. She joined the ancient teachings with everything she knew and formed Modern Tantra.

I purchased her first book, Beyond Sex: Tantra and remember reading a statement which said "Tantra is the ultimate love affair with yourself and all of your existence. In the process of igniting your internal flame, you come to experience all ordinary moments as extraordinary experience". I love that and wholeheartedly believe that to live a happy, fulfilling life every day you need to see the extraordinary in the ordinary. I did not know at the time, but this was to be the beginning of a huge journey..........my meditation and massage had added a huge change in my way of thinking about myself, life, love and relationship but now there was more. These things have all combined to become that 5% that I was missing.

I watched and followed Tanja and her teachings for a while and wanted to learn more. I read her next book "Riding the Phoenix", which was both heart-breaking and inspiring at the same time. This woman had gone through the most enormous traumas and yet had come through the ashes to produce an amazing program for people to follow which would help them to change just about anything about their lives they wanted to. The teacher in me stirred again and at this point and I knew I had to learn more and that one day too I would be teaching this work and inspiring people to grow and change their lives. Incredible insight now that I look back because that is exactly what I am doing four years later!

Evolution One
Robyn

So here I was signed up to study a Tantra course online with a group of other people I didn't even know and a woman living on the other side of the world. This was a first for me, an online course, as I usually preferred to attend classes and be more hands-on. The timing of the live sessions was really bad for me as it was 2am and really not a great time to be trying to focus and learn.

I did enjoy listening to the recordings though and I had read Tanja's book Riding the Phoenix so was aware of the many breath practices and the incredibly powerful role they could play in healing and being able to make change. What I loved the most about Tanja's work, and still do, is that it is simple, but it works. I am not sure what it is about us as humans, but we tend to make things so complex at times and stripping back to simplicity is a real key to success. For me, the simplicity of this work had great parallels with the simplicity of the Huna principles, so I really wanted to learn as much as I could.

Interestingly though, I believe I did sit on the outer of this group, only making a few Facebook comments on our private group page. Many people in the group seemed to have such enormous issues and trauma in their lives to deal with and in comparison, my life had been a breeze. I felt a bit like a fake being a part of a coaching program that was dealing with such big stuff. I did not want to comment about other people's issues as I had no idea if what I said would be helpful or not.

While I was probably not the best student at doing everything, I was asked during this level, I was diligent in learning the practices and was interested in the five elements of concept, learning, practise, experience and commitment. My commitment let me down during this time as I still sat on the outside and approached this as another way of thinking rather than a way of life. This was definitely going to change in the following levels as I began to realise my own patterns and strategies and that just because my issues were not huge they still needed attention.

Evolution Two
Robyn

When the opportunity came up to continue for another six months onto the next level of the program, there was absolutely no choice to be made, I was in. I was loving this program more and more and being a part of a group of like-minded people and being a part of their journeys felt great. I had a tribe to belong to and I realised that my contributions and my life and what I had achieved could be an inspiration to others.

In each level, there would be breath practices to do each day and so now I was really on board, my commitment to the practices increased. My all-time favourite breath practice is Dynamic Conscious Breath, I guess because I can do it anywhere and at any time fairly inconspicuously, so it is instantly effective. Every night I still do this breath practice before I go to sleep.

There were five main areas that stood out for me during this level. The first was to realise that every practice we did was a meditation and helped to keep you totally present. Whether I was doing Static Hold and bringing focus to my body or doing spontaneous stretching for flexibility or being in nature I was totally present to that moment. The second area was to look at my patterns and what strategies I was using to stay in these patterns.

One of my patterns which I had realised during Level One, was that I was a peacekeeper. My husband and I rarely argued because more than likely I didn't say what I was really feeling, I was avoiding confrontation but not honouring myself and what I thought and felt about the situation. Being free to say how I really felt changed so much for me, I didn't feel locked in or shut down anymore, I was free to be me. This pattern was something I had imposed on myself, maybe I thought I was being a good wife or a better partner, I'm not sure but I am definitely a better person now that I allow myself to be open and honest about my thoughts and feelings.

Another great exercise we did was to contemplate control by writing down where you are trying to control things in your life and the strategies you use to keep and gain control. The third area was to write a values list and then to look at whether I was using my values to make decisions in my daily life. If you are not living your values, you will be living in conflict. My initial list was Love and Passion, Family, Happiness, Gratitude, Honesty and Knowledge. The fourth area was learning to insource, which means using your body wisdoms to know what you need, or feeling into your body as your body has all your answers. The seven body wisdoms include Survival, Enjoyment, Power, Love, Expression, Clarity and Wholeness and relate to different areas of your body, similar to chakras. The last area for me, was the importance of having a gratitude mantra that you speak aloud or to yourself every day and that it was something you really felt and meant, not just a string of words. Mine is: "I am grateful for all that I am and all that I have".

What I loved more and more about Tanja and the course as it unfolded were the fantastic one-liners that were absolute pearls of wisdom that came out of Tanja's mouth during each call.

My Level Two favourites were:

All energy is neutral until you put a charge on it.

Love is a self-state…love yourself first.

Balance is the ability to allow and create.

Inhale what is, exhale what will be.

Evolution Three
Robyn

The major focus for me during level three was concentrating on self-care as it is vital to have a solid foundation of care to give you the freedom to be able to do other things in life. If you have a handle on self-care, then you are fully resourced and can have passion and purpose to do whatever you want. The basic four to concentrate on at this moment were Sleep (to have a dark room in which to sleep and be getting to bed at a reasonable hour and having no electronic devices distracting you from sleep), Hydration (at least two litres of water to clear any inflammation in the body), Exercise (spontaneous stretching for fluidity and a natural way to move, walking and other exercise that is enjoyable and preferably outdoors so you can also connect with nature) and Healthy Food (fresh, nourishing food to make the body feel alive and restricting intake of alcohol, coffee and other stimulants).

Another task to be done in this level was to write a needs list, which was a list of all the things in your life that you needed and how often you needed them to feel like you were flourishing, not just surviving. My list included nine things which were seeing or speaking to at least one member of my family each day, being near or driving past the river or ocean a few times a week, singing, playing or listening to music every day, eating healthy food, attending my boxing class each week, learning or researching new things, socialising with friends and family weekly, feeling the sun on my skin and being outside in the fresh air and making love or snuggling with my husband.

The list of needs also gives you a clue to your values as your needs and values work together. My values list remained fairly similar to my first original list although I re-named them with more appropriate words. It now reads Family, Support, Passion, Gratitude, Integrity and Curiosity.

At this stage, we also discussed relationship, sexual chemistry, emotional trauma and how each of the practices could help you to heal. We also did 30-day challenges, which make you feel absolutely bullet-proof when you finish them because many people don't trust themselves to do what they say they will and this exercise blows that trust issue out of existence.

The power of words was also another "aha" moment for me as I did not realise how much power your words are to your subconscious and how easy it was to change. For example, "I have to go and do the dishes" sounds like a chore and has a negative context whereas I can go and do the dishes takes away that negative, dark energy and it becomes a positive, thing you can do! I never used to like ironing as I felt it was a chore too but when I switched my mindset to thinking that I loved seeing my husband go to work in his newly ironed clothes, then I actually enjoyed it, it gave me pleasure. The fact that we can heal ourselves both physically and emotionally is the greatest thing we can learn as human beings and to have the tools to do so is the absolute key to living a life of pleasure every day. At this stage, I was learning the tools to be able to handle any situation that life could possibly give me and that felt very powerful indeed.

Level Three one-liners:

Fear keeps people stuck

If you can't say no, then you can't say yes

Evolution Four
Robyn

YOUR AWAKENED PASSION AND PURPOSE

When you realise your spiritual connection to something bigger than you and you have self-care and self-management, relationships, needs and values in place then you are able to see your true passion and purpose in life. Passion is full arousal and creates an excitement in you that you just love, it is something you just have to do. It is our patterns that hold us back, things like making excuses, self-sabotage, feeling sorry for ourselves, not feeling good enough, fear of failure etc.

One valuable exercise we did was to write a bucket list of all the things we wanted to see and do in the world, a bucket list is what inspires you but can also reveal to you some of your patterns. For example, you could have said I want to travel to America next year but I can't afford it or I can't get time off work, these are excuses!!!! If you really want to travel you can save the money, get extra work, use frequent flyers, you can be expansive in your outlook rather than closed off and shut down.

The key to moving forward and to creating change is expansion not contraction, when we expand we open up to all possibility when we contract we get smaller and close down.

Purpose and passion require action, so another exercise that helps you to move forward is to write things down and prioritise them. We were all asked to make a Bullet Journal which consisted of daily tasks, monthly tasks and things that you would like to do in the future.

If you have outstanding things that you want to achieve, for example, cleaning out the cupboards, paying the bills, weeding the garden, losing weight etc this creates anxiety which in turn creates overwhelm.

When you are in overwhelm it is difficult to move forward, so by breaking the task down into small manageable steps you will be successful in moving forward to your desired goals. By writing things down, you can see what needs to be done and there is great satisfaction in marking things off your list. Success breeds success so if you make small, achievable goals then you will succeed. The most important thing to moving forward is to take action...forget the head talk, forget the explanations, no blah, blah, blah!!

My passion and purpose in life is to be a Mum, hence my number one value is family. My daily decisions are based on what is good for my family and what my family needs at the time. My mission in life is to educate, teach and support others to live the life they choose to live. Perhaps that is why I was a primary school teacher for 25 years and now I get to step back into that role that I loved so much for so long. Life is awesome!

Level Four one-liners:

Your devotion to self is PARAMOUNT

Fear kills PASSION

Knowledge and Awareness equal Potential

Actions that you take equal Change

Evolution Five
Robyn

YOUR COURAGEOUS ACTION

Life mastery is a custom journey into the things that are important to you. These things are different for everybody and they are not necessarily grand or world-changing, but they are yours and you own them. It is the ability to check into your life and the decisions you are making and to notice when you are out of alignment.

Level Five was essentially a re-cap of where you are in committing and devoting to yourself and by using the practices in your life as a part of making changes not just as a checklist. By using the tools learnt in the program, I can look at my life at any stage and ask myself, is my life exactly how I want it to be and if not why not? I would feel into my body wisdoms and ask myself, am I having the family, tribe, finances experience I want? Do I have creativity and a good sex life? Am I confident and living bravely? Am I open-hearted and compassionate to myself and others? Am I speaking my truth and not my triggers? Am I intuitive and insightful, can I see and feel what is happening in me and correlate that to what is happening outside of me? Life mastery is based on absolute self-trust.

Most importantly we have no control over our base emotions, we want to feel them but not be paralyzed by them. We want to be current with our feelings and know the difference between how it feels for real or as a trigger. Triggered fear is overwhelming anxiety, a looping pattern of thoughts, whereas primal fear is an instant feeling of do I need to be worried, am I in danger. Your chemistry can be instantly changed by taking a few deep breaths. With the help of all the tools we have, we practise 'being brave', feeling the fear and doing it anyway!!

When you are fully insourced, you are totally self-sufficient and find it easy to be in relationship and community. You check in multiple times a day to how you are feeling and whether or not a breath practice (alternate nostril breathing, fire-breath) or other practice like stretching, eye rolling, or hydration might make you feel better.

"There is no perfect life to be had, what there is, is the evolution of yourself to make life more fun, more graceful, more of what you need and want it to be" Tanja Diamond

Coaching
Robyn

I was absolutely chuffed to be accepted into the coaching program as one of only four participants and excited to be on this journey. I was going to be sharing my knowledge again and this excited me, just the same way that teaching did for me all those years ago. Over the next six months there were many things I learned that would help me to be a better coach but here are my top ten:

- You MUST walk your talk

- The biggest gift you can give your coaching candidates is that they see you as a work in progress and still learning yourself.

- Take everyone to the basics, meet them where they are, they need self-awareness

- People are drawn to you for who you are and what you offer

- The work your client does outside the sessions with you is where the actual change takes place

- Be a storyteller, tell your clients your story, vulnerability as well as successes, your clients trust you more when you are real and open with them

- Create neutrality in yourself, they need to have their own experience, not a version of yours.

- Celebrate and point out client's successes

- You need to be both kind and bad ass

- Have a format and make it your own

One task we had to complete to achieve our certification was to do 50 hours of coaching, that is, ten hours of coaching with five different people. The sessions were all recorded and sent to Tanja for feedback. It took me back to University days where I had a marker sitting in the back of the classroom analysing my teaching style and ability to relate to and manage the student's behaviours. It felt scary at times waiting to hear Tanja's feedback but invaluable at the same time as I wanted to be the best I could be. I was very happy with the results of my five coaching candidates, and although there were some challenges they all made significant changes to their lives.

Going to Seattle for the Coaches retreat in July last year was a highlight for me, as I was finally getting to meet Tanja and the other girls in person. The Skype coaching sessions we had were amazing, to be live on a call with them was a first for me after the previous five levels had been only recordings. Now, I was meeting them in person, spending a few days together in the beautiful mountains outside Seattle and working together on our coaching mission statements, and other documentation as well as doing some live coaching sessions, with clients we had never met. It was fabulous, and we achieved so much in those few days and formed a bond together as the High Speed Evolution Coaching Team.

WHAT'S HAPPENING NOW?

I would have to say that I couldn't be happier with my life. I work part-time with my husband in our business, manage our unit on Air BnB and Stayz, look after my aging Mum and also babysit my three beautiful granddaughters from time to time. I enjoy going out to lunch, chatting and shopping with my daughters and catching up with my son over lengthy phone conversations or when he comes home to visit. I sing in an amazing choir and have also formed a duo with a friend and we do charity performances all over the Coast.

I have my own coaching clients and have also started doing my Lomi Lomi massage again. My life is full and busy, but I make time for myself too, enjoying my weekly boxing classes, walks on the beach with friends and family, coffee dates and the occasional trip to the Day Spa. My husband and I make it a priority to travel overseas at least once a year, to enjoy some relaxation time and to experience another culture together. I still do my breath practices and get out in nature every day.

The death of my father eighteen months ago was a huge tragedy and very sad time for me and for the rest of the family. He was my hero and the other love of my life and I was grateful to have spent the last three days of his life, lying beside each other, holding hands and singing to him. Life is full of ups and downs, but it is how we handle the ups and downs that makes us who we are. I am grateful to have the tools of the High Speed Evolution program as I am able to live each day to the fullest, to experience all the emotions that come my way but to live my life the way I choose to and to experience joy and gratitude on a daily basis.

CONCLUSION

Free Gift for You

Amazing right! I had so many emotions the first time I read through their chapters. I could see my past struggles in so many different parts, how about you? I cried and cheered with joy as well as they broke through old patterns!

Love a coach and want to tell her how amazing she is or learn more about her coaching, see us at

www.EvolutionCoaches.com

Since the writing of this book things have changed for all of us of course, now being masters of change and all LOL. The big motion for me is bringing on four new coaches and three of them men and a fifth one coming up the ranks in Evolution Four right now. That's pretty exciting stuff and I look forward to that new experience of having men in our tight knit group.

I will put another book together with the next set of coaches so look forward to that!

I also came to realize that I will only be certifying about 40 coaches in my lifetime. Each coach represents a great deal of my time and we all stay connected and there is ongoing support and retreats to attend and enjoy!

And as a final parting gift I would love to offer you a free Video Mini Master Class on Living Your Best Live Ever, simply head to this link and grab the free ebook and the videos will be sent to you via email.

http://bit.ly/2GyUTkT

Interested in finding out how you stack up on Your Personal Freedom Journey, take the free assessment here

http://bit.ly/2ihER3A

Visit us on Facebook at Evolution Coaches and say hello and let us know how you enjoyed the book! The coaches would love to hear from you.

If you want to experience the group coaching program you just read about I typically start a new Evolution One- Your Life Unleashed once to twice a year. Please contact me for more information at Tanja@tanjadiamond.com

We wish you the very best in all you do and remember,

BE AMAZING!

Tanja

About
Tanja Diamond

Tanja Diamond is an Innovator in Transforming and Expanding the limits of Human Potential.

As a Lineage Tantra Master, Peak Experience Expert, Master Coach Trainer and Business Alchemist she has been called "Bold, Unorthodox and Revolutionary" with unique and creative approaches for getting results at warp speed. Her passion to explode the box and find ways to get the undoable accomplished inspires her clients to new heights of astounding personal evolution and radical courage.

Tanja is a three-time International best-selling author and Speaker who works worldwide awakening consciousness in all aspects of life and business.

The architect of two highly effective and successful technologies, Modern Tantra-The Six Foundations of Integrated Living and High Speed Evolution- The Five Evolutions to Life Mastery, she guides you to Your Personal Freedom where you will experience "Integrated Intelligence" a source of Mastery in Your Being.

Tanja is currently offering two coach certification programs, Evolution Coaches and Neo Tantra Certified Coaches.

Other bestselling books by Tanja Diamond

Beyond Sex: Tantra, a practical guide for extraordinary living

Riding The Phoenix- The ultimate guide to get untuck in life love and money

Ebooks-

Conscious Breath

The Art of Getting Unstuck

Tantra Foundations

Healing Through Tantra

Video Master Classes-

Your Life Unleashed

The Art of Tantra

Tanja has private coaching, workshops, business masterminds, online courses and other products and events and is available for interviews, speaking engagements and your private groups.

She currently has a podcast/videocast series with her friend Lyric called, Lyric and Tanja Exposed, on Itunes, Youtube and Facebook.

Find her on Facebook- Tanja Diamond Unleashed

Reach Tanja at tanja@tanjadiamond.com or call her at 206-276-2735

Made in the USA
Lexington, KY
27 May 2018